BLACKJACK

TAKE THE MONEY AND RUN

by
Henry J. Tamburin

Research Services Unlimited
Casino Gambling Book Publisher
P.O. Box 19727
Greensboro, NC 27419

i

Address all inquiries to the publisher:
Research Services Unlimited
P.O. Box 19727
Greensboro, NC 27419

Manufactured in the United States of America

ISBN: 0-912177-09-8
Library of Congress catalog card number: 94-92109

Fifth printing, April 1997

The material contained in this book is intended to inform and educate the reader and in no way represents an inducement to gamble legally or illegally.

Preface

My goal in writing this book is to teach you how to consistently walk away from the blackjack tables with profits. This consists of a game plan of knowing how to play, how to bet, and most importantly, when to quit. It's the latter that usually separates the winners from the losers.

Part of the contents of this book first appeared in *Henry Tamburin on Casino Gambling* and in various articles I have written about blackjack winning techniques. All of this material, including the notes from my blackjack courses and seminars have been combined, revised, expanded, and brought up to date for this book.

There is no question that blackjack can be beaten by the skillful player. This has been proven beyond a doubt through mathematical studies and in the practical playing experiences of skillful players. I personally have won more money playing blackjack over the past 25 years than I have lost. You will discover that the main theme throughout this book is that you must learn to discipline yourself to quit a playing session once you have generated a profit. This sounds trivial but it always amazes me to witness blackjack players losing their hard earned table profits. What matters is not how much profit you have setting on the tables but rather how much you have in your pocket when you exit the casino.

This book begins with an explanation of the basic playing rules for blackjack as it is played in jurisdictions throughout the country. This includes, besides the traditional Nevada and Atlantic City games, the new dockside casinos in Mississippi, riverboats in Illinois, Iowa, and Louisiana, and the numerous blackjack games found in casinos on reservations. You'll also learn in this chapter which playing rules are more favorable for the player.

Chapter Two explains why blackjack can be beaten and why it's different "mathematically" than the other casino games. The correct basic playing strategies are explained and presented in the form of tables and charts in Chapter Three. You'll also find suggestions on how to learn this playing strategy in an efficient manner.

Chapter Four contains a winning strategy for the novice player that does not involve card counting. This unique card scanning technique for single and double deck games can be readily learned and implemented by a beginning player to give them a slight edge over the casino. This chapter also contains a recommended betting strategy for the recreational player who can not or will not learn the techniques of card counting.

Chapter Five will introduce you to the techniques of card counting. An intermediate level strategy is presented that involves using the running count for sizing your bets. The latter is coupled with a win progression betting scheme that results in a betting methodology that I have called the streak count.

Chapter Six presents a powerful, advanced level playing strategy that will teach you how to use the true count for betting and for strategy deviations. This is the playing strategy that I have successfully used to win money from the casinos. Learn the techniques in this chapter, and you will become a world class blackjack player.

No book on blackjack is complete without a

discussion of risk. By understanding and respecting risk (Chapter Seven), you will be better able to handle the sometimes up and down fluctuations in your bankroll which are unfortunately inherent in the game of blackjack.

After having experienced my first barring incident from an Atlantic City casino many years ago, I can appreciate the fact that if the casinos <u>don't</u> let you play it really doesn't matter how well you play. Therefore, in Chapter Eight I review some common sense guidelines on how to implement your playing skills without fear from the casino bosses.

Chapter Nine contains my philosophy about playing blackjack, namely, I play to win money and when I'm ahead, I'm gone ("take the money and run"). Hopefully, the techniques that I have perfected over the years to discipline myself to quit a winner will also work for you.

Chapter Ten contains somewhat unrelated but important topics for blackjack players. Here you'll learn about dealer tipping, how blackjack teams operate, the typical casino countermeasures toward card counters, an overview of newer and sometimes controversial playing techniques, and a summary of the new playing options that casinos have recently introduced to stimulate more interest in blackjack.

Many individuals have contributed to the success of this book. I acknowledge the first group of individuals by name in Chapter Five for their contributions to our understanding of the game of blackjack. Due to their studies and writings, understanding blackjack has always been a continuous learning experience for me. Secondly, I acknowledge my friend and partner, Dick Ramm who did all the computer studies to help me develop the strategies presented in this book. Lastly, I must acknowledge the readers of my books, columns and former students for challenging me to improve my knowledge of blackjack.

Chris Schneider deserves my thanks for typesetting this book, Ben Jordan for the cover design, Bob Tate for suggesting the title and finally my wife Linda, for spending countless hours helping me proof this book.

I'd be most interested in hearing from the readers of this book (pros and cons) so that I can continuously improve it. Please send your written comments to the publisher (Research Services Unlimited), my attention.

Whether your goal is to learn how to play blackjack, improve your game, or become a world class player, I wish you much success in your quest to "take the money and run."

Henry J. Tamburin

TABLE OF CONTENTS

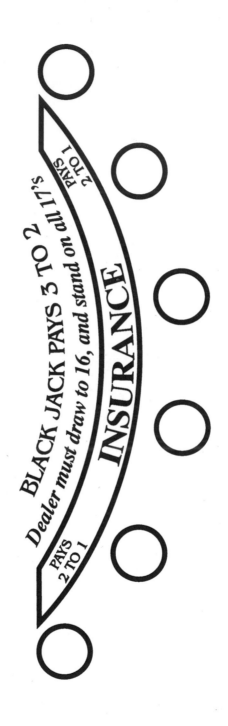

BLACK JACK PAYS 3 TO 2

Dealer must draw to 16, and stand on all 17's

PAYS
2 TO 1

INSURANCE

PAYS
2 TO 1

1
Basic Playing Rules

Your first task in becoming a winning blackjack player is to thoroughly understand how the game is played.

Objective

The objective of the casino game of blackjack is simply to beat the dealer by having your cards total higher than the dealer's without your total exceeding 21. It is not, as some people think, to get as close to 21 as possible.

Card Values

The cards from 2 through 10 count face value. All picture cards count ten. The ace counts as 1 or 11 at the player's discretion.

Example: K,4 = 14   10,6 = 16
           ace,3 = 14 (or 4)   3,6,5 = 14

Soft and Hard Hands

It is important to distinguish between a soft hand and a hard hand. A soft hand in blackjack is a hand which contains an ace counted as 11.

Example: ace,4 = soft 15   2,ace,3 = soft 16
          ace,8 = soft 19   ace,2,4 = soft 17

A hard hand is a hand which either does not contain an ace, or if it does, the ace counts as 1.

Example: ace,5,10 = hard 16   ace,2,3,9 = hard 15
          5,10 = hard 15   ace,6 = soft 17

Card suits (spades, diamonds, etc.) have no meaning in blackjack.

Table Layout

The typical blackjack layout is crescent shaped, covered with a colored felt with white lettering, and with enough space to accommodate six or seven players. Each of the squares (or circles) on the layout represents a player's wagering spot. Casino chips (or checks) are used for wagering and the dealer will exchange your cash for chips at the table. Simply attract the dealer's attention before the deal, place the cash on the table outside of the betting square (or circle) and ask the dealer for "chips please." The dealer will count the cash, give you the equivalent amount of chips and place the cash in the drop box located to the right of the dealer. The cash "drops" into a locked metal box.

Casino Personnel

Every blackjack table has a trained dealer who conducts the game. Their job is to deal the cards and conduct the game by established rules, pay off winning bets, collect losing bets, exchange cash for chips and ensure the game is operatcd in a professional manner. The many blackjack tables are located in an area known as a pit. Several blackjack tables are supervised by floor persons, who in turn report to the overall pit supervisor, more commonly known as the pit boss.

Chip Denominations

In general casinos standardize their chip denominations and colors. The usual colors for the different denomination casino chips are:

$1.00	white	$25.00	green
$2.50	pink	$50.00	orange
$5.00	red	$100.00	black
$10.00	brown	$500.00	purple
$20.00	yellow		

The above colors are in fact the standard colors for chips used in Atlantic City casinos. Casinos in other locations may use different colors or, in fact, silver dollars in place of the one dollar casino chip. In any event, chips have the amount that they are worth imprinted on them so there is never any confusion about this.

In casino terminology, five dollar chips are often referred to as "nickels" and twenty-five dollar chips as "quarters."

Table Limits

All blackjack tables have an allowable minimum and maximum bet. For example, at the $2, $3 and $5 tables, the maximum bet is usually $500 or $1,000. At $10 and higher tables, the maximum bet is usually higher. The minimum/maximum bets allowed for each blackjack table is posted at the table for players to see (usually on a placard that sets on the table to the dealer's right).

Some casinos are regulated to a maximum bet of $5 per hand (notably Colorado and Iowa casinos). Others set their minimum/maximum bet depending upon casino policy and floor traffic within the casino.

Numbers of Decks

The casinos can use one or more decks of cards at their blackjack tables. Usually, if a single or two (double) decks are used, they are dealt by hand. When four, six, or eight decks are used, the cards are dealt from a device known as a dealing shoe. As you will see later in this book, the casino advantage over the average blackjack player increases with the number of decks used.

Mechanics of Play

At the start of a game the dealer will shuffle all the cards and ask a player to cut the cards with a plastic cut card. Why the card cutting? First of all, it reinforces the idea of an honest game to the player. And secondly, card cutting psychologically is good for the game because the player supposedly cuts his or her own luck.

The dealer completes the cut and then places the cut card at some predetermined place in the deck(s) of card(s). Every casino maintains a policy as to where the dealer is permitted to place the cut card. Usually, the cut card is positioned one-half to two-thirds from the top card. (The depth of the cut is known as the penetration). This means that from one-half to two-thirds of the cards will be put into play. When the cut card appears, that round of play is completed and then all the cards are reshuffled.

After the shuffle and cut, the first (top) card is normally placed by the dealer in the discard tray. The removal of this top card from play is known as burning. The value of the discarded or burned card is usually not shown to the players unless requested by a seated player.

Each player must place a wager prior to the dealer dealing the cards. After all wagers are made, the casino dealer will deal the cards starting from their left to right. Each player in turn will receive a card until each player and the dealer are dealt two cards. One of the dealer's cards is face up, the second face down. The latter is known as the dealer's hold card or down card.

Normally when casinos use single or double decks of cards, the dealer will toss the cards to the players either both face down or one card face up and one face down. In these types of games, the players are permitted to touch or hold the cards. In games using multiple decks of cards dealt from a shoe, the player cards are usually dealt face up. In this situation, players are *not* permitted to touch or handle the cards.

After all players and the dealer have received their initial two cards, the dealer will ask each player in turn (starting from his/her left or "first base" position), if they want additional cards to improve the total of their hand. You can ask for as many cards as you like, but if the hand total exceeds 21 it is an automatic loss regardless of the outcome of the dealer's hand. If you request additional cards, they will be dealt face up. You may also stand with the original two card total or exercise several player options such as doubling down, pair splitting, and taking insurance. After all the players complete their turns, the dealer then must play out his/her hand.

Busting

Whenever your hand or the dealer's exceeds a total of 21, this is known as busting. If you bust, it is an automatic loss. If the dealer hand busts, all player hand totals which have not busted are automatic winners.

Stiff Hands

Hands which total 12 through 16 which can be busted by drawing one card are generally known as stiff hands. These hands occur quite often and usually pose the most difficulty for a novice player.

Pat Hands

Hands that total 17 through 21 are generally known as pat hands. These are the hands in which a player would usually "stand pat" and not draw additional cards.

Blackjack

When a player or dealer's first two dealt cards total 21, he or she has received the best hand possible in the game - a blackjack or natural.

Player Hand Signals

There is usually very little conversation between the players and dealer because of the pace of the game. To maintain this pace, and for the benefit of observers who monitor the activity at each table, you must use hand or card signals to indicate to the dealer whether or not you want to stand (no further cards required), or hit (receive additional cards). In games in which you are not permitted to touch the cards (in multiple deck games) and you want to draw additional cards to improve your hand total, you signal this to the dealer by making a beckoning or scratching motion with your finger on the table layout. If instead you are satisfied with your hand total and do not want additional cards, signal this to the dealer by waving your hand over the cards. In doing so, you are relaying to the dealer that you want to stand with your card total.

In games in which the players can handle the cards (i.e. player cards dealt face down), you indicate standing by tucking the cards under the chips wagered on the hand. If you want a hit or additional draw cards, the proper signal is to take the cards in your hand and "scratch" the table with them.

Players can draw as many additional cards as they wish. Keep in mind, however, that if the total of the cards exceeds 21, the player is an automatic loser regardless of what happens to the dealer hand.

Dealer's Play

The playing out of the dealer's cards is regulated by the rules of the game. The dealer must stand if the initial two cards total 17 through 21. Some casinos, in particular in downtown Las Vegas and northern Nevada, dealers will hit soft 17 (A,6). This is not as favorable for the player compared to casinos in which the dealer must stand on soft 17.

If the dealer's cards total 16 or less, they must continue to draw cards until the hand totals 17 or more. If the dealer busts (exceeds 21) then all the players remaining in the game are winners. If your hand and the dealer's have the same total, this is known as a draw, tie, or push, and you neither win nor lose. If the dealer's total (17 through 21) exceeds your total, you lose. Likewise, you win if the total of your hand exceeds the dealer's total.

Player Options

In addition to the basic decision to hit or stand, players have certain important options for playing out their hand. When properly exercised, these options are an important part of an overall strategy to end a playing session with a profit and then take the money and run!

Pair Splitting

If the initial two cards dealt to you have the same

value (eg. 8,8; 9,9; Ace,Ace) you may split the hand into two hands. Statistically, you'll receive a pair about 144 hands out of every 1,000 hands (ca. 14%).

In games in which players are not permitted to touch the cards, the proper signal for pair splitting is to simply place the same value chip(s) next to (not on top!) the original wager in the betting circle. Do not separate or touch the cards; the dealer will do this.

In hand held games, when you want to pair split, simply place the cards face up on the table above your initial wager (closest to dealer) and then make the secondary wager next to the initial wager.

By pair splitting you have converted the initial hand into two independent hands and also doubled your wager. Each of the two hands must be played separately. Should you receive a card of like value to the initial two split cards, most casinos will allow you to resplit a third and if it happens a fourth time. For example, if you split a pair of sixes and receive a six as the draw card to the first hand, you may make another wager and split the pair of sixes again. In this case the player would have three hands with three wagers, each hand having a single six.

You may request as many draw cards as you wish to each split hand until you are satisfied with the hand total. The exception is splitting aces. In this case, casinos universally (with very few exceptions) will only permit one draw card to each split ace. The reason for the latter is because allowing unlimited drawings to split aces would work too much to the player's advantage.

The following is an example of how pair splitting works in a multiple deck shoe game where all the player cards are dealt face up.

You wager five dollars in a multiple deck game and receive a 7,7 versus a dealer upcard of 2. In this situation, splitting the original hand of 14 (7,7) into two hands of 7 is an advantageous move. To initiate the pair split, place an additional five dollars next to the original five dollar bet in the betting area (this can be done anytime - even before your turn). When it becomes your turn to play out the hand, the dealer will automatically separate the two sevens and deal one card to one seven. Let's assume it was a 10. You want to stand with a 17, so you wave your hand over the cards. The dealer now automatically deals a card to the second seven. Let's assume it's a 2. The hand now totals 9. You want to hit so you scratch your finger on the table indicating to the dealer to give you another card. The card dealt is a 9. The hand now totals 18 and you wave your hand over the cards indicating you want to stand. The net result of this pair splitting is that the original five dollar wager on the 14 (7,7) has now become a five dollar wager on 17 (7,10) and an additional five dollar wager on 18 (7,2,9). Remember, however, that just because you receive a pair doesn't mean you always split them. There are specific pairs that are to your advantage to split, and the decision to do so depends upon the value of the cards and the value of the dealer's upcard. (More about when to split shortly).

Doubling Down

This option allows you to double your original wager in favorable situations in return for receiving one and only one draw card. To signal double down in hand held games, simply toss your cards face up on the table and place an equivalent (or less) amount of chips next to your original wager. The dealer will give you your draw card face down and tucked under your chips. You may peek at the down-card or wait until the dealer reveals it at the end of play. In games where the player's cards are dealt face up, signal doubling down by placing an equivalent amount of chips (or less) next to your original wager. The dealer will give you one draw card and place it face up and perpendicular to the original two cards.

Casino rules vary as to when a player may double

down. The best rules for the player are unrestricted doubling down which means a player can double down on any two initial cards. Some casinos only allow doubling if the initial two cards total 9, 10 or 11. This is not as favorable as the unrestricted doubling down. Normally casinos only allow a player to double down after the first two dealt cards. Once a player asks for a hit, the double down option is no longer available (some casinos, however, allow doubling after 3 or 4 draw cards as a come-on).

The most important rule as far as doubling down is concerned, is the ability to double-down after pair splitting. This is a most favorable option for the player and is a much better deal than casinos that do not allow this option.

Most casinos allow players to double for less as long as the double down bet meets the minimum bet requirement for the table. For example, if you had wagered $10 at a $5 minimum bet table, you could, if you wish, double down for $5. However, because doubling down is such a very favorable option for the skilled player, it is to your advantage to always double down the maximum allowed (equal to original wager).

Surrender

The playing option known as surrender is not widely offered by casinos. It is a favorable player option when used properly.

When a player surrenders he/she forfeits one half the initial wager and is no longer involved in that round of play. Players must initiate the surrender option after receiving the initial two cards and before drawing any cards. Normally a player cannot surrender after pair splitting.

There are two versions of surrender, late and early. In late surrender, a player can surrender as long as the dealer does not have a blackjack. In early surrender, the player may surrender his/her first two cards *before* the dealer checks for a blackjack. Obviously early surrender is highly favorable because it allows the player to save half the wager against a dealer's blackjack. Unfortunately, most casinos do not offer early surrender and late surrender is only sporadically offered.

Insurance

When the dealer's upcard is an ace, the dealer will momentarily stop the game and ask all the players if they wish to buy insurance. In essence, the insurance bet is a side bet in which you can wager one-half of your original bet (for that hand), that the dealer's hole card is a picture card or ten. Note that the insurance bet has nothing to do with the original bet. In fact, the term insurance is a misnomer. To initiate the insurance bet, you place an amount of chips equal to one half your original wager on the insurance line (located above the player betting areas - see blackjack table diagram). When the dealer turns up his/her hold card and it's a ten or picture card, the dealer has blackjack and the insurance bet is a winner at a 2 to 1 payoff.

Some casinos allow the player to take even money when the player has a blackjack and the dealer has an ace showing and asks for insurance. When a player in this situation asks for even money, he/she will be paid the amount equal to the initial wager before the dealer checks his/her hole card. Asking for even money is exactly the same as the player insuring his/her blackjack.

Dealers will check their hole card by carefully peeking at it so that players do not see the card value. Some casinos also require their dealers to also peek at their hole card if their upcard is a ten. Many casinos have also installed a special device on their table which allows the dealer to check the hole card without peeking. The device, known as a maxtime reader, consists of a window, mirrors and light and is used with a special deck of cards in which the value of the aces, tens and picture cards are imprinted sideways on the card so it can be seen by the dealer.

Example of Insurance Bet
     You wager five dollars and are dealt a 10 and 8. The dealer's upcard is an ace. Before any player has an opportunity to complete his hand, the dealer stops the game and asks "insurance?" The dealer waits until all the players who want to make an insurance bet have done so. Assume you decide to take insurance. To do so, you would place a two and one-half dollar chip in front of your original bet (closest to the dealer). After all the insurance bets are made, the dealer will peek at his/her downcard. Let's assume it's a ten. The dealer will turn over the ten to show the players the blackjack. Your original five dollar bet on the hand is lost. However, the insurance bet wins and is paid off at five dollars (2 to 1 payoff). The net result is that you break out even. In the event the dealer's hole card is any other card than a ten or picture card, the insurance bet is automatically lost.
     In general, the insurance bet, including the even money on a player blackjack, is *not* a good bet unless you have some knowledge as to the ratio of tens and picture cards to other cards left in the remaining cards to be played (i.e. you are card counting). I'll have more to say about the insurance bet in the next sections.

The Payoff
     After the players and dealer complete their hands, the dealer must compute each player's total (except those that busted) and compare the total with his/her total to determine the payoffs.

     A) If the dealer's total is 17 through 21
               - players lose their wager if their total is less
                    than the dealer's
               - players win an equal amount (1 to 1 payoff)
                    if their total is greater than the deal-
                    er's total
               - players tie if their hand is equal to the

dealer's and the wager belongs to the player.

B) If the dealer's total exceeds 21 (i.e. the dealer busts) then all players who are still in the game (everyone that didn't bust) will be paid off at 1 to 1.

C) The wager for all players whose total exceeds 21 (busted) is automatically lost even if the dealer subsequently busts.

D) All player blackjacks are paid off at 3 to 2. Thus a two dollar wager will be paid off at three dollars. A five dollar wager will be paid at seven dollars and fifty cents, a ten dollar wager at fifteen dollars, etc.

E) The insurance bet is paid off at 2 to 1 if the dealer's hole card is a ten or picture card.

Blackjack Miscellany

The following pointers should minimize your nervousness when starting to play blackjack in a casino.

1. Always look for the placard which sets to the dealer's right on the table, describing what the minimum bet is for that table.

2. To convert cash to chips simply wait until the dealer completes a round of play, then place your cash on the table and announce loud and clear "Chips Please." The dealer will convert your cash into chips.

3. You must make your wager before the dealer begins to deal. Once the dealer begins to deal the cards, you are not allowed to place a bet for that round.

4. At no time should you touch your original wager, remove part of your wager, or add additional chips on top of your wager (this may be construed as cheating) until after the bet is paid.

5. At no time should you touch or handle the cards in games where the cards are dealt face up. The dealer is responsible for manipulating the cards.

6. The player seated to the far right (left of the dealer) is known as "first base." The player seated to the far left (right of dealer) is known as "third base." The player seated in third base is known as the "anchor" player.

7. Player blackjacks are paid off immediately at 3 to 2 except if the dealer's upcard is an ace or ten. In this case, the payoff occurs immediately after the dealer turns over the hole card (unless, of course, the dealer has a blackjack too).

8. Blackjack always beats a 21 hand. Also, drawing tens or picture cards to split aces is not a blackjack, and will lose if the dealer has a blackjack. Remember! A blackjack occurs only when the *first* two cards *total* 21.

9. In blackjack games where the cards are dealt face down, pick up the cards with one hand only.

10. Make sure you give all hand signals from behind your chips in the betting circle. Your hands should never extend beyond your wager (except when making the insurance bet).

11. After you finish playing blackjack, dealers will sometimes ask you to "color up" your chips. The

dealer will stack your chips in the middle of the table and then give you higher denomination chips in place of the lower ones you may have had.

12. Always remember to use hand signals rather than verbally stating "I stand or hit." The only allowable verbal signal is to indicate "surrendering" a hand.

13. Do not ask fellow players for advice on how to play a hand. This can be annoying. If you need advice, you shouldn't be playing in the first place.

14. Casinos will normally allow a player to play two hands. In this case, the usual casino policy is that you must wager at least double the minimum bet on both hands.

15. If you need to take a break from the tables for personal reasons (bathroom, make a telephone call, find your spouse, etc.), you can ask the dealer to hold your seat. The dealer will place a clear plastic disc in your betting spot indicating to other players that the seat is reserved. Normally, the casinos will hold your spot for 10-15 minutes. (If you do leave the table for a break, be sure to take your gaming chips with you).

Now that you know the basics of how to play blackjack, let's begin to learn how to beat the game and then take the money and run!!

2

Why Blackjack
Can Be Beat

It's important for you to understand why the game of blackjack can be beat. With this knowledge it then becomes easier to learn "how to do it."

The casino offers several games to the public which include, beside blackjack, the games of craps, roulette, baccarat, big six wheel and, of course, the slot machines. Blackjack is quite different mathematically from the other games. It is a game based on what mathematicians call dependent trial processes as opposed to the games of craps or roulette, which are called independent trial processes.

In the game of craps, there are certain probabilities which can be calculated for rolling a certain number with a pair of dice. For example, the odds against rolling a 7 are 5 to 1. These odds are constant and do not change, regardless of what happened to be thrown on the previous dice rolls. The dice, if you wish, have no memory. The odds are independent of what has occurred in the past. The same holds true for the game of roulette. The odds against any number appearing on a particular spin of the wheel are 37

17

to 1. These odds remain the same regardless of what numbers appeared in previous spins of the wheel. It is a game of independent trial processes.

One characteristic of all "independent trial processes" casino games is that mathematically, with an honest game, there are no playing or wagering systems that can overcome the casino's advantage in these games. A player always has a negative expectation (the casino has the edge).

Blackjack, on the other hand, is different. It is a game based on dependent trial processes. The odds against winning a particular hand are quite dependent upon what cards were played in previous hands. Thus the odds of winning a hand are constantly shifting from dealer to player (compare with craps or roulette where the odds are constant).

It should be obvious to you that if the mix of the cards previously played has a bearing on winning or losing, then by knowing this mix you could alter your bets or playing strategy to maximize your chance of winning a particular hand. Thus, blackjack is a game of skill, not chance, and by using certain skills you could swing the odds in your favor.

In addition, because the game of blackjack is mechanical (fixed set of rules) it is quite amenable for analysis on a computer. There are over 500 possible situations with your cards and the dealer's. In each instance, you can double down, hit, stand, split, etc. Which is the best possible move for any one of these situations? How can you tell?

By calculating expectations for an infinite number of games, or by simulating the play of a large number of games and observing the results, a computer can be used to determine the mathematically correct play for any particular combination of player hand and dealer upcard.

Thus blackjack offers the skillful player an opportunity to have a positive expectation (i.e. the player has a mathematical advantage of the casino). This is the only casino game where this could occur!

Given this mathematical fact that a skillful player can beat the game of blackjack, why then would the casinos offer such a game to the public? After all, they are in the business to make money. The reason is quite simple. Remember, it's the skillful player who can win. And to be skillful, a player must devote a certain amount of study and practice to learn these skills. Fortunately for the casinos, the majority of players are not willing to put in the time or effort required to learn these skills. So, while the majority lose, a relatively small handful of skillful players win. Which is fine, because someone has to lose the money won by the skillful players!

There are other reasons why players continue to lose at a game that can be beaten. During my years of experience as a player and gaming instructor, I have heard of all kinds of excuses as to why someone can't win at blackjack. I call these excuses "blackjack myths". These misconceptions about the game are unfortunate because in most cases these are the reasons or excuses given by a player for not learning how to win. So as to eliminate all final excuses, I will now proceed to answer the four most often quoted myths.

"It's impossible to win at blackjack. It is a game of luck." Entirely false. Blackjack is a game of skill, not chance and it is the *only* casino game in which you can enjoy a long term mathematical advantage over the casino with skillful accurate play.

"You must have a photographic memory or be a mathematical genius in order to win." Not so. Anyone with the ambition and desire to improve his/her game can learn, with practice, the basic blackjack playing strategy and simple techniques to track the cards as they are played. No photographic memory or mathematical background is required.

"It is impossible to count cards with 4 or 6 decks." Counting cards in a 4 or 6 deck game admittedly takes more mental effort than doing the same with a single deck. But it is not impossible; all that is required is practice.

"You need a tremendous bankroll to win appreciable amounts." Even if you have a small bankroll you can still win a lot. The key is to increase your bets in proportion to your bankroll. As you begin to win, your bankroll will increase, thus your bet size will increase proportionately and the amount you will win will increase.

Let us now get into the specifics of how to win at blackjack. What's required is a game plan which consists of the knowledge of how to play the hand, how to manage the gaming bankroll, and most importantly knowing when to take the money and run!

Development of Winning Blackjack Strategies

The development of a winning blackjack playing strategy was accomplished by simulating the game of blackjack on a computer. It is important to understand how this is done to appreciate the final set of "playing rules."

Let us assume for the moment that you are playing blackjack in a casino, you are dealt a 7,8 and the dealer shows an upcard of 8. You must now make a decision, "Should I try to improve my hand of 15 by drawing an additional card, or should I stand on 15?"

Even without the use of a computer you could determine the correct play for this hand by doing the following: Arbitrarily deal a 15 and a dealer's upcard of 8, then play one hundred or more mini-games in which you draw to the 15. Then complete the dealer's hand. After each of these mini-games record the won/lost results. The process should now be repeated, except you would stand on 15. At the conclusion of these mini-games, compare the results of hitting or standing on a 15 versus dealer's 8. The better percentage play is the one which shows the greatest number of wins.

Notice that determining the correct play requires comparing the number of wins or losses for two (or in some instances, three) player options. This is the identical principle that is used in computer simulation analysis, except the computer will simulate and compare many thousands of blackjack hands at very high speeds.

In all cases, the optimum, or mathematically correct playing strategy is the one which either

1. Shows the greatest profit or
2. Shows the smallest loss.

To amplify this point, the computer simulation results for the above hand of 15 versus a dealer upcard of 8 follows:

Situation: Dealer has upcard of 8. You have a two-card total of 15 (8,7).

If you hit a hand of 15 (8,7) with a dealer upcard of 8, you stand to lose 71% of the hands and win 29% of them.

If you stand, then you can expect to lose 76% of the hands and win 24% of them.

Note that a hand of 15 versus a dealer upcard of 8 is in either case a losing hand. If you stand, you can expect to lose 76% of the hands; if you hit, you'll lose 71% of the hands. The optimum strategy in this case would be to hit, because it results in 5% less losing hands.

This concept of losing less always seems to confuse the novice player. It is important to remember that in a game of blackjack it is impossible to win every hand. In fact computer studies show that all player hard hands of 12 through 17 are overall losing hands in that you will not win more than 50% of these hands. All blackjack players have to live with this fact, and the best you can do in a losing situation is to minimize the loss. Losing as little as possible is just as important as winning as much as possible.

My associate, Dick Ramm, and I have studied the game of blackjack using computer simulation for over 20 years. Dick is a computer whiz and he has helped me develop correct playing and counting strategies for many different blackjack games. He was a pioneer of developing one of the first over the counter software programs (The Amazing Blackjack Machine) that allow players to simulate playing thousands of hands of blackjack on their personal computers. Dick's eyesight and hearing has failed him over the years and he is no longer able to study the game of blackjack on his computer. I am indebted to him for the tremendous help and assistance he has given me over the 20 years we have known each other. Besides assisting me in the development of blackjack playing strategies, Dick is co-author with me of the classic book, *Winning Baccarat Strategies.*

At this point in this book you should have an understanding of how the game of blackjack is played and why it can be beaten by skillful play. Let's now begin our journey to become a world class player by first learning the correct playing strategies.

3

Basic Blackjack
Playing Strategies

The information presented in this chapter forms the basis for all the playing strategies presented in this book. You must commit the time and effort that's required to learn this basic strategy to become a winning blackjack player.

First, let's make sure you understand how the casinos create their mathematical advantage (or edge) over the players. It's really quite simple. The rules stipulate that all the players must play out their hands *before* the dealer plays out his/her hand. And in the course of the players playing out their hands, if their hand exceeds 21 or busts, guess what? That's right, the player is an automatic loser regardless if the dealer subsequently busts. The fact that the casino automatically wins all player bets that have busted creates their edge.

Suppose a player takes the position that he/she will mimic the dealer's playing strategy and always hit a hand that totals 16 or less and stand on 17 or more. The casino's edge over such a playing strategy is about 5.5% because the

dealer always automatically wins when a player's hand busts.
In reality the casino's edge over most blackjack
players who don't mimic the dealer's playing strategy could
be higher or lower depending upon the specific playing
strategy used by the player. The casino's advantage over the
"worst" blackjack player can approach 15% whereas the
smart player who uses the basic strategy presented in this
chapter will reduce the casino's advantage to virtually 0.

An additional factor that effects the casino's advantage in blackjack is the house rules. Different rules modify
the casino's advantage either positively or negatively. The
effects of rule changes is summarized in the chart below.
Numbers with a positive sign indicate the percent advantage
to the casino. Numbers with a negative sign are player
favorable rules.

Single Deck	No advantage
Two Decks	+0.35%
Four Decks	+0.52%
Six Decks	+0.58%
Eight Decks	+0.61%
Dealer hits soft 17	+0.20%
Double on 9,10 and 11 only	+0.10%
Double on 10 and 11 only	+0.25%
Resplit aces	−0.05%
Double down after splitting	−0.13%
Late surrender	−0.05%
Early surrender	−0.62%
No splitting of aces	+0.18%
Double on 3 or more cards	−0.21%
Six card automatic winner	−0.15%

Using the above information, it is possible to estimate the casino's advantage for any given set of rules. For
example the casino's advantage in a 4 deck Atlantic City
game with late surrender is as follows:

4 deck game	+0.52%
Double down after pair splitting	-0.13%
Late surrender	-0.05%
Casino's Advantage	+0.34%

Several Mississippi Gulf Coast dockside casinos offer two deck games with doubling after pair splitting. The casinos advantage is:

2 deck game	+0.35%
Double down after pair splitting	-0.13%
Casino's Advantage	+0.22%

In the casinos in Reno, Nevada, single decks are used but the dealer hits soft 17 and doubling down is allowed on 10 and 11 only. The casino's advantage is:

Single deck	0
Dealer hits soft 17	+0.20%
Double on 10 and 11 only	+0.25%
Casino's Advantage	+0.47%

Another interesting fact from the above chart is that the casino's advantage increases as the number of decks increases. Notice that the biggest change of +0.35% occurs when the casino goes from a single to double deck game. The casino's advantage tapers off as the number of decks approaches eight (to 0.61%). In fact, if the casino were to use an infinite number of decks, their casino advantage would be about 0.70%.

The table on page 26 summarizes the typical playing rules for several casino locations. These rules can change so use this as a guide. For up-to-date information on blackjack playing rules and conditions in general, you need to consult either Arnold Snyder's *Blackjack Forum* or Stanford Wong's *Current Blackjack News* (see Suggested Reading).

TYPICAL PLAYING RULES

(For up-to-date playing conditions, consult Arnold Snyder's *Blackjack Forum*, Stanford Wong's *Current Blackjack Newsletter* or Dalton's *Blackjack Review*).

Las Vegas Strip	•Dealer stands on soft 17 •Doubling permitted on any two cards •Multiple splits allowed •Doubling after pair splitting not allowed
Las Vegas Downtown	•Dealer hits soft 17 •Doubling permitted on any two cards •Multiple splits allowed •Doubling after pair splitting allowed •Mostly single deck
Atlantic City	•Dealer stands on soft 17 •Doubling permitted on any two cards •Multiple splits allowed •Doubling after pair splitting allowed •Mostly 6, 8 deck games; some 4 decks
Mississippi Gulf Coast	•Dealer stands on soft 17 •Doubling permitted on any two cards •Multiple splits allowed •Doubling after pair splitting allowed •Mostly 2, 6, and 8 deck games
Northern Nevada	•Dealer hits soft 17 •Multiple splits allowed •Doubling on 10 and 11 only •Doubling after pair splitting not allowed •Mostly single deck

By now you are probably wondering why the casino's advantage increases with the number of decks. The first reason is because the probability of obtaining a blackjack is *less* in multiple deck games than it is for single deck games.

To explain this we have to do a little arithmetic. First let's figure out what the probability is of getting an ace as your first card dealt to you from a single deck. Since there are only four aces in a single 52 card deck, the probability of getting the ace as the first card is simply the ratio of 4 divided by 52 (4/52). OK, but to get a blackjack you need to have the second card dealt to you be a ten value card. When the dealer gets ready to give you the second card, he or she is dealing from a 51 card deck (remember, the first card dealt from a 52 card deck was your ace). From these 51 cards, only 16 have the value of ten (the four tens, four jacks, four queens and four kings). Thus the probability of the dealer giving you a ten as your second card is simply the ratio 16 divided by 51 (16/51). To arrive at the probability of the dealer giving you a blackjack by dealing you an ace first, then a ten from a single deck is simply the two ratios multiplied together - 4/52 times 16/51 equals 0.024.

But there's another possibility of getting blackjack. The dealer could, instead, give you a ten as the first card (not an ace) and an ace as your second card. Using the same analogy as above, the probability of this occurring is also 0.024 (16/52 times 4/51). Thus your overall probability of being dealt a blackjack as the first two cards (either ace,ten or ten,ace) is simply 0.024 plus 0.024 equals 0.048.

The number that's important is the 0.048. Because now you must go through the entire exercise for a six deck game and compare the calculated overall probability to the 0.048 calculated for a single deck game. If you do this exercise, you'll find that the overall probability of getting a blackjack in a six deck game is 0.0237 plus 0.0237 equals 0.047.

The above probability for getting a blackjack in a six deck game (0.047) is less than the probability of getting blackjack in a single deck game (0.048). Thus using simple arithmetic, you can mathematically calculate why the single deck game is better for the player than a six deck game.

The increase in the casino's advantage with more

decks of cards is one of the reasons why casinos have gone to multi-deck games. Another reason is that the frequency of player favorable situations for blackjack card counters is less in multiple deck games than single deck games. We'll have more to say on this in the chapter on card counting.

The following sections explain the basic blackjack playing strategies for every player option. Tables that summarize the strategy are in Appendix I.

Hard Hitting/Standing Strategies

Of all the blackjack plays you will have to make, standing or hitting will occur the most frequent. And understanding when to hit those 12 to 16 hands and when not to will often be the difference in leaving the tables a winner or loser.

The rules for hitting or standing on a 12 through 16 hand have been clearly defined through millions of computer simulated hands. Whenever you are dealt any of the following hands, you should hit or stand according to the following rules:

If you have a hand that totals 13, 14, 15, 16 and the dealer's upcard is 2, 3, 4, 5 or 6, you should STAND.

If instead the dealer's upcard is 7, 8, 9, 10 or ace, you should HIT your 13, 14, 15, 16 hands.

If you have a hand that totals 12, then STAND if the dealer's upcard is 4, 5, 6 and HIT your hand if the dealer's upcard is 2, 3, 7, 8, 9, 10 or ace.

Here are some simple rules which you can use right on the tables to help you make the right play. First, let's define two kinds of blackjack hands, namely a stiff hand and a pat hand. Stiff hands are all the 12 through 16's. The term 'stiff' means those hands that could exceed 21 with a one card draw. A 'pat' hand is one in which a player normally stands pat or doesn't hit. The 17 through 21 hands are known as the pat hands.

When you play blackjack, it is very easy to determine

if the hand dealt to you is either a stiff or pat hand. Obviously, if your hand totals 12 through 16, it's a 'stiff', and if it's a 17 through 21, you have a 'pat' hand.

You always see one of the two dealer's cards (the upcard) and for the purpose of this exercise, always make the assumption that the dealer's downcard or hole card is a 10. This, in fact, is not such a bad assumption to make since there are four times as many tens in a deck of cards (all the 10's, J, Q, K's count ten) than any other value card.

With the assumption that the dealer's downcard is a 10, you can now determine whether the dealer has a stiff or pat hand. If the dealer's upcard is a 2 through 6, he or she probably has a 12 through 16 hand which is a stiff. Likewise, if the dealer's upcard is a 7 through 10, he or she probably has a 17 through 20 or a pat hand.

Once you've determined the stiff/pat nature of your hand and the dealer's, use this simple rule to determine whether to hit or stand.

Player stiff against dealer stiff...STAND.
Player stiff against dealer pat...HIT.

For example, you're dealt a 7,8 (15) and the dealer upcard is a 4. Your hand is a 'stiff'. Assuming the dealer's downcard is a 10, then the dealer has a potential 'stiff' (10,4=14). With a 'stiff' facing a 'stiff', you should stand.

Suppose you are dealt a 9,7 (16) and the dealer upcard is a 7. Here we have a player 'stiff' against a potential dealer pat hand. With a 'stiff' facing a 'pat', you should hit.

Learning to recognize hands as stiff or pat will make learning the rules for when to hit or stand very easy. Following the stiff/pat rules will allow you to make the correct play in all cases except one, and that's when the player has a 12 and the dealer upcard is a 2 or 3. In this case, the player should hit even though it is stiff against stiff.

Keep in mind that the above rules only hold for player hand totals of 12 through 16 when the hand either doesn't contain an ace or if it does, the ace counts as one (known as hard hands). If you have a 12 through 16 hand which contains an ace counted as 11, the above rules should NOT be used. (Thus you follow the rules if you are dealt a 10,6 (16) or 10,5,ace (16) but not if you are dealt an ace,5 (16).) Hands which contain the ace counted as 11 are special and are called soft hands. Strategies for soft hands are explained on the next page.

You must always keep in mind the following fact of blackjack. You will receive hands that total 12 through 17 about 43% of the time and overall these are losing hands irregardless of what the dealer's upcard is. In other words, computer analysis of each hand vs. different dealer's upcard shows that you will always have less than a 50% chance of winning the hand no matter if you hit or stand (with just one exception, standing on 17 vs. dealer 6). The hard standing and hitting strategies if followed, will minimize your losses in a losing situation. This is an important point to remember: 12 through 17 hard hands are overall losers and the best we can do with these hands is to minimize our losses by following the basic strategy.

Dealers' Upcard

Understanding the frequency at which the dealer will bust based on his/her upcard will help you understand the above hitting and standing strategies. Extensive computer analysis reveals the frequency at which the dealer will bust or exceed 21, depending upon the dealer's upcard, is as follows:

Dealer's Upcard	2	3	4	5	6	7	8	9	10	ace
% Bust		35	37	40	42	42	26	24	23	23	17

The dealer's worst upcards are 2 through 6 because he/she must hit these hands no matter what the value of the hole card is and his/her probability of busting is high (one exception is the possibility of the dealer having a 6 upcard and an ace as a hole card).

As long as the dealer must keep hitting, your chances of winning improve. The main advantage the dealer has over you is that you must go first, and if you bust, the bet is automatically lost, even if the dealer's hand subsequently busts too. Thus your best percentage play is to stand on low value hands (don't risk busting) whenever the dealer shows a low value upcard and a correspondingly high probability of busting (with one exception, hit a hand of 12 whenever the dealer shows a 2 or 3).

On the other hand, if the dealer's upcard is a high value card, such as 7, 8, 9, 10 or ace, the dealer is most likely to have a 'pat hand' (17 through 21). In this case, your best percentage play is to keep hitting until the hand totals 17 through 21.

Soft Hand Strategies

Blackjack hands which contain an ace that count as an eleven are called soft hands. An example is ace,5 (16); ace,3,3 (17); and ace,ace,4 (16).

As a general rule, a player should never stand on any soft hand that totals 17 or less. It doesn't matter what the dealer's upcard is...never stand with a soft 13, 14, 15, 16 or 17. The logic for never standing on these hands is simply based on the fact that a soft hand between 13 through 17 can not bust or exceed 21 by drawing a card since the ace, due to its dual role, can always be counted as one. For example, if a player holds an ace,5 (16) and draws a 9, the player's hand now totals 15 (not 25). Thus you always have a chance to try to improve your soft hand total without risking breaking the hand.

There is still another playing option to consider with soft hands and that's the option of doubling down (explained further in next section). Too many blackjack players ignore doubling down on soft hands which is unfortunate since in some cases it is by far the optimum playing strategy.

Generally, a player should always double down on soft hands from 13 through 18 when the dealer's upcard is a 5 or 6. Why? Simply because with a 5 or 6 upcard, the dealer has the greatest chance (about 40%) of busting his hand. And with this knowledge, it is to a player's advantage to put as much money on the table as possible. This you can do by doubling down. Thus, if you hold an ace,5 and the dealer's upcard is a 5, this is the opportune time to double your bet because of the dealer's high probability of busting. You actually have two chances of beating the dealer in this situation. First, you could improve the hand by drawing a small card (an ace through 5) which would give you a 17 through 21 hand. And even if you aren't lucky enough to draw a small card but instead draw a 6 through 10 (which will give you a 12 through 16 hand) all is not lost because the dealer still has a high probability of busting in which case you'll win the hand anyway.

There's still one more rule to master regarding soft hands and that has to do with hitting and standing on soft 18. Believe it or not, the optimum playing strategy for a soft 18 against a dealer's 9,10 or ace upcard is to hit your hand. Many players would never think to hit what seems to be a good hand of 18 *but* you will lose more hands by standing on 18 against a dealer's upcard of 9, 10 or ace than if you hit the hand. To put it another way, a player total of 18 just isn't good enough against a dealer's upcard of 9, 10 or ace.

If you hold a soft hand of 19 through 21, the optimum playing strategy is simply to stand no matter what the dealer's upcard is, with one exception. In single deck games, double down soft 19 vs. dealer 6.

Double Down

Doubling down allows you, in most cases, to maximize your profits in a winning situation. It is an offensive strategy that when properly exercised, will lead to many winning sessions.

Again, through computer studies, we can determine which initial player's hand vs. a particular dealer upcard has a greater than 50% chance of winning. If you are in a situation where your chances of winning the hand are better than the dealer's, why not increase your bet to win more? You can by learning when to double down.

The following is a summary of the correct double down basic strategy for multiple decks and doubling after pair splitting. (The use of single decks and exclusion of doubling after splitting will change certain decisions).

- If your two card hand totals hard 11 (e.g. 7,4), double down if the dealer's upcard is 2 through 10 (hit if the dealer's upcard is an ace).

- If your two card hand totals hard 10 (e.g. 6,4), double down if the dealer's upcard is 2 through 9 (hit if the dealer's upcard is a ten or ace).

- If your two card hand totals hard 9 (e.g. 6,3), double down if the dealer's upcard is 3 through 6 (hit if the dealer's upcard is any other value).

- If your two card hand totals soft 17 or 18 (e.g. A,6 or A,7), double down if the dealer's upcard is 3, 4, 5 or 6).

- If your two card hand totals soft 15 or 16 (e.g. A,4 or A,5), double down if the dealer's upcard is 4, 5 or 6.

- If your two card hand totals soft 13 or 14 (e.g. A,2 or A,3), double down if the dealer's upcard is 5 or 6.

The use of a single deck affords the player more opportunities to double down. This includes

doubling 11 vs. dealer ace
doubling 9 vs. dealer 2
doubling 8 vs. dealer 5,6
doubling A,8 vs. dealer 6
doubling A,6 vs. dealer 2
doubling A,2 and A,3 vs. dealer 4.

Also, if doubling down after pair splitting is *not* allowed, you should also double down on 4,4 vs. a dealer's 5 and 6.

The complete double down strategies are presented in the tables in Appendix I.

Let's take a moment and explain the reasons for these double down strategies.

Your two card hands that total 9, 10 or 11 should be doubled because you have an excellent chance of obtaining a pat hand by drawing a ten value card. As discussed in the previous section, soft doubling is recommended when the dealer has a high probability of busting (dealer has a low value upcard). Remember, that you can only double down on your first two cards. Once you draw a third card to any particular hand, the double down option is no longer available.

In an earlier section, a computer method used to determine the "best" playing strategy was discussed. It depended on comparing the percentage of hands won or lost on standing or hitting a particular hand versus dealer's upcard. Doubling down must be evaluated in a different manner and for the benefit of the readers who wish to know how this is accomplished mathematically, an example is provided.

To evaluate if doubling down is the better strategy versus hitting, the amount of money wagered per hand must be considered. For example, computer analysis shows that:

If you hit a hand of 11 versus a dealer's 8, then you can expect to win 61% of the hands and lose 39%. Assuming you wager $1 per hand, the net dollar won per hand would be: (61%–39%) x $1 = 22 cents per hand.

If on the other hand you double down on 11 versus an 8, you can expect to win 59% of the hands and lose 41%. Note that you will win less hands doubling than by hitting. This is because if you receive a low value card by hitting you have an opportunity to improve the hand by further drawing. If you double you receive only one card and cannot draw additional cards. Assuming you wager $1 per hand, the net dollar won per hand by doubling down would be: (59%–41%) x $2 (extra double down bet) = 36 cents per hand. Clearly doubling gains you fourteen cents per hand (36–22) as opposed to hitting.

Similar calculations are used to determine the soft doubling rules.

Pair Splitting

In general, a hand should be split vs. an alternate playing strategy such as standing or hitting if it meets one of the following criteria:

1. You will win more, on average or
2. You will lose less, on average or
3. You turn a losing hand into a winning hand.

Let's give a few examples to explain.

Assume you are dealt a 9,9 and the dealer upcard is a 6. We know from extensive computer studies that if you stand you can expect to win 64% of the hands and lose about 36%. This means if you bet $1 per hand, playing this hand 100 times, you can expect an average profit per hand of $64–$36 divided by 100 = 28 cents. Quite obviously this is a winning hand.

Assume, however, that you decide to split the 9's. Again, through computer studies, we find that you now stand to win 60% of the hands and lose 40%. Your long term profit potential per hand is now 2 (because you are doubling your bet on pair splitting) times $60−$40 divided by 100 = 40 cents.

Note that by pair splitting your profit per hand is greater by 12 cents. Clearly pair splitting, in this case, is the best percentage play because it will win you more on average (criteria No. 1).

Let's now take a look at how you can minimize your losses in a losing situation by pair splitting. Assume you are dealt a pair of 7's and the dealer upcard is a 2. If you stand with your 14 (7,7), you can expect to win 36% of the hands and lose 64%. Your net loss per hand is $64−$36/100 = 28 cents.

If instead you split the 7's, you can expect to win 45% of the hands and lose 55%. Your average loss per hand is now 2 x $55 − $45/100 = 20 cents. You're still in a losing situation but you've cut your loss rate down from 28 cents/hand to 20 cents/hand. Clearly, pair splitting gains you 8 cents and is the best percentage play to make in this situation (criteria No. 2).

The final example shows how pair splitting can turn a losing hand into a winner. You're dealt a pair of 7's, the dealer has a 6 upcard and you stand. You can expect to win, on average, 42% of the hands and lose 58% for a net loss per hand of 16 cents. By pair splitting you stand to win 52% of the hands and lose 48%. Your net profit per hand is now 8 cents. You've turned a 16 cents per hand deficit into an 8 cents per hand profit. That's smart strategy (criteria No. 3).

The above analysis can be used for all combinations of player pairs and dealer upcard and the result is the following mathematically correct pair splitting strategy for multiple deck games that allow doubling after pair splitting.

Pairs	Split when dealer's upcard is
2,2	2 thru 7
3,3	2 thru 7
4,4	5 and 6
5,5	NEVER SPLIT
6,6	2 thru 6
7,7	2 thru 7
8,8	ALWAYS SPLIT
9,9	2 thru 9 except stand on 7
10,10	NEVER SPLIT
ace,ace	ALWAYS SPLIT

In casinos that do *not* allow doubling after pair splitting, the following modifications must be used.

Split 2,2 vs. dealers 4-7
Split 3,3 vs. dealers 4-7
Do not split 4,4
Split 6,6 vs. dealers 3-6

In a single deck game, the proper pair splitting strategy is as follows:

	Dealer Upcard
	(doubling after pair splitting not allowed)
2,2	3 thru 7
3,3	4 thru 7
4,4	Never
5,5	Never
6,6	2 thru 6
7,7	2 thru 7
8,8	Always
9,9	2 thru 6 and 8,9
10,10	Never
Ace, Ace	Always

Modify the above for casinos that allow doubling down after pair splitting as follows:

2,2; 3,3; 6,6	2 thru 7
4,4	4, 5, 6
7,7	2 thru 8

Surrender

The surrender option when available allows the player to forfeit half of the original wager and give up the opportunity to play out the hand. Once a player draws a third card the surrender option is no longer available. Also, if the dealer has a blackjack, the player may not surrender.

Not too many casinos offer surrender. For those that do, you would be surprised, in fact amazed, at the types of hands that players surrender. Actually, knowing what hands to surrender is strictly based upon the following: if you want to forfeit half of your bet you should only do so when the casino's advantage against you is greater than 50%. Those hands are as follows:

Late Surrender (multiple decks)
16 vs. dealer upcard 9, 10, ace
15 vs. dealer upcard 10
Do not surrender 8,8

Late Surrender (single deck)
16 vs. 10
15 vs. 10
7,7 vs. 10

Early surrender was once offered in the Atlantic City casinos. This option allowed a player to surrender before the dealer checked for a blackjack. This is an extremely favorable player option with a potential gain of 0.6%. Because of this, the casino industry in Atlantic City successfully lobbied for the discontinuation of this option. In the event this very favorable option is revived, here are the hands to surrender:

Early Surrender
17 vs. dealer upcard ace
16 vs. dealer upcard 10, ace
15 vs. dealer upcard 10, ace
14 vs. dealer upcard 10, ace
13 vs. dealer upcard ace
12 vs. dealer upcard ace
7 vs. dealer upcard ace
6 vs. dealer upcard ace
5 vs. dealer upcard ace
Do not surrender soft hands

Insurance

For the average blackjack player (who is not card counting), insurance is a poor bet which should never be made. Simple mathematics will clearly show why.

In a six deck game, for example, there are 312 cards of which 96 are ten value and 216 are non tens. If the dealer shows an ace upcard, he/she will have a ten value card in the hole on the average of 96 out of 311 hands. If you took the insurance bet every time the dealer shows an ace then the following would happen.

96 times you win 2 to 1 on the insurance bet = +192 chips
215 times you lose your 1 chip insurance bet = −215 chips

Your net loss is 23 chips (−215 + 192) for every 311 chips wagered and the casino's advantage is about 7%. Making a bet with a casino advantage of 7% is not a smart play.

Now what about the special case of making an insurance bet or taking even money when you are dealt a blackjack hand. Most casino gaming "experts" (dealer, floor persons, fellow players and friends included) would *always* recommend that you insure (or take even money) your blackjack because you must win. The reason for this is shown in the following chart which lists all the possible outcomes when you insure a blackjack (assume initial wager of 2 chips).

	Situation	Player Outcome	Net
1.	Dealer has blackjack. Player does not take insurance.	Blackjack - a push	-0-
2.	Dealer does not have blackjack. Player takes insurance.	Blackjack wins 3 chips 1 chip insurance lost	+2 chips
3.	Dealer has blackjack. Player takes insurance.	Blackjack a push Wins 2 chips on insurance	+2 chips
4.	Dealer does not have blackjack. Player does not take insurance.	Blackjack wins 3 chips	+3 chips

Note that if you have a blackjack and take insurance (situations 2 & 3) regardless of whether or not the dealer subsequently has blackjack, you must win 2 chips.

So on the surface, making the insurance bet (or taking even money) looks like a can't lose proposition. However, what the experts don't tell you is that based on some simple mathematical calculations a player who does *not* insure a blackjack stands to win *more* than 2 chips per hand on average. In fact, your guaranteed 2 chips win per hand turns out by calculation to be about 3.9% *less* than what you would be winning per hand on average if you never insured your blackjack. Therefore the statement "you must win" should be amended to read, "you must win *less*, when you insure or take even money with a blackjack."

There are situations however, when the insurance bet is a smart play. Since you are betting that the dealer's hole card is a ten value card, your chances of winning this bet are greater if the balance of cards still to be played contain an excess of ten value cards than usual. In fact, if the ratio of non-ten value cards to ten value cards in the unplayed cards is 2 to 1 or less, then you stand to win more money than you will lose when you make the insurance bet. Of course the only way you will ever know this is by card counting or keeping track of the ten and non-ten value cards as they are played. So the bottom line for making the insurance bet can be stated very simply. *Unless you are card counting, never make the insurance bet or take even money even if you have a blackjack.*

Basic Strategy Tables

The basic strategy rules can be presented in the form of a table which makes them easier to learn.

The full matrix of strategy decisions for single and multiple decks along with different playing rules is presented in Appendix I. The following tables are a condensed version of the popular single and multiple deck games found in the majority of casinos.

Before you begin to study the basic strategy tables, let us make sure you understand them.

The two variables that determine how you should play your hand are the value of the dealer's upcard and the kind and total of your hand. For example, how should you play the following hand?

Player dealt: Ace, 3. Dealer's upcard is a 2.

Look at Table I and go down the column headed Your Hand to A,3. Now read across. It states: double on 5 or 6, otherwise hit. What this means is that you should double down on your A,3 (soft 14) hand only if the dealer's upcard is a 5 or 6. If it isn't you should then hit the hand. Since the dealer's upcard is *not* a 5 or 6, you wouldn't double down rather *hit* the hand.

TABLE I
Multiple Deck (4, 6, 8) Basic Strategy
Double down on any two cards
Double down after pair splitting permitted

| | Playing Strategy vs. |
Your hand	Dealer's Upcard
8	Always hit;
9	Double on 3 to 6. Otherwise hit.
10	Double on 2 to 9. Hit on 10, A.
11	Double on 2 to 10. Hit on A.
12	Stand on 4 to 6. Otherwise hit.
13	Stand on 2 to 6. Otherwise hit.
14	Stand on 2 to 6. Otherwise hit.
15	Stand on 2 to 6. Otherwise hit.
16	Stand on 2 to 6. Otherwise hit.
17	Always stand.
18	Always stand.
A,2	Double on 5,6. Otherwise hit.
A,3	Double on 5,6. Otherwise hit.
A,4	Double on 4 to 6. Otherwise hit.
A,5	Double on 4 to 6. Otherwise hit.
A,6	Double on 3 to 6. Otherwise hit.
A,7	Double on 3 to 6. Stand on 2, 7 or 8. Hit on 9, 10 or A.
A,8 to A,10	Always stand.
A,A	Always split.
2,2	Split on 2 to 7. Otherwise hit.
3,3	Split on 2 to 7. Otherwise hit.
4,4	Split on 5,6. Otherwise hit.
5,5	Never split. Treat as 10 above.
6,6	Split on 2 to 6. Otherwise hit.
7,7	Split on 2 to 7. Otherwise hit.
8,8	Always split.
9,9	Split on 2 to 6, 8 or 9. Stand on 7, 10 or A.
10,10	Always stand.

Never take insurance.

If surrender is offered, surrender 16 vs. 9, 10, Ace and 15 vs. 10.

If doubling down is *not* allowed after pair splitting, then use the following pair splitting rules.

Split 2,2 vs. dealer's 4 thru 7

Split 3,3 vs. dealer's 4 thru 7

Never split 4,4

Split 6,6 vs. dealer's 3 thru 6

TABLE II
Single Deck Basic Strategy
Double down on any two cards
Double down after pair splitting *not* allowed

Your hand	Playing Strategy vs. Dealer's Upcard
8	Double on 5 to 6. Otherwise hit.
9	Double on 2 to 6. Otherwise hit.
10	Double on 2 to 9. Otherwise hit.
11	Always double.
12	Stand on 4 to 6. Otherwise hit.
13 to 16	Stand on 2 to 6. Otherwise hit.
17 to 21	Always stand.
A,2 to A,5	Double on 4 to 6. Otherwise hit.
A,6	Double on 2 to 6. Otherwise hit.
A,7	Double on 3 to 6. Stand on 2, 7, 8. Hit on 9, 10, or A.
A,8	Double on 6. Otherwise stand.
A,9	Always stand.
A,A	Always split.
2,2	Split on 3 to 7. Otherwise hit.
3,3	Split on 4 to 7. Otherwise hit.
4,4	Same as 8 above.
5,5	Same as 10 above.
6,6	Split on 2 to 6. Otherwise hit.
7,7	Split on 2 to 7. Stand on 10. Otherwise hit.
8,8	Always split.
9,9	Split on 2 to 9 except 7. Stand on 7, 10 or A.
10,10	Always stand.

Never take insurance.

If surrender is available, surrender 16, 15 and 7,7 (14) vs. dealer 10 upcard.

If doubling down is permitted after pair splitting. Then use the following pair splitting rules.

Split 2,2 vs. dealer's 2 thru 7
Split 3,3 vs. dealer's 2 thru 7
Split 4,4 vs. dealer's 4, 5, 6
Split 6,6 vs. dealer's 2 thru 7
Split 7,7 vs. dealer's 2 thru 8

If a casino is using two decks, modify the table as follows:

Hit 7,7 vs. dealer's 10
Hit 11 vs. dealer's Ace
Hit 8 vs. dealer's 5 or 6
Stand A,8 vs. dealer's 6

Learning Basic Strategy

Too many blackjack players think they know the basic strategy by heart. Luckily for the casinos, this is not so. You must take the time to learn this strategy so that you always make the correct decision.

Here are some techniques that you can use to help learn the strategy.

Put the strategy on index cards. Put the strategy for each player hand and dealer upcard on index cards. Put the player hand on one side, for example 8,8 vs. dealer 6, and the correct playing decision from the tables on the other side of the index card (in this example you would write "always split."). By rewriting the strategy on the index cards, this alone will help in the learning process. Once you have the cards prepared, start to go through them one by one. Look at the hand plus dealer upcard side of the card and then from memory recite the strategy. Flip the card over to check your answer. Put all the cards that you gave an incorrect answer to the side and spend more time relearning the proper strategy.

Try to reproduce the strategy table. I've included a blank strategy table in Appendix II. Make copies of it, then try to reproduce the strategy table from memory. Check your answer with the tables in Appendix I.

Simulate playing situations with a deck of cards. This is how I first learned the basic strategy some 25 years ago. Take one card and throw it up on the table. This is the dealer's upcard. Then take 2 cards and put them on the table. This is your hand. Decide what is the correct strategy and if necessary check your answer. Repeat using the same dealer upcard but throw down 2 (or more cards) to represent your hand. Keep practicing this way using different dealer upcards.

Practice with a computer. There are a host of handheld calculator/computers that allow you to practice your blackjack strategies. In addition there are several computer software programs for PC's that will do the same. An inexpensive and very good software program that will teach you the basic playing strategy is Dr. Thorp's Mini Blackjack. Please see the Suggested Reading section at end of book for additional details on this and other programs.

Bring a strategy card with you. You should carry a pocket reference card that contains the basic strategy when you play. If you forget what the correct playing decision is for a particular hand, refer to the card. You should not use this card, however, as a substitute for memorizing the basic strategy.

For those interested, I market a durable, laminated, pocket reference card that contains all the correct playing decisions. Details about the card are summarized at the end of this book.

I can not overemphasize the importance of learning the basic strategy. You will not win every hand by following the basic strategy. It will, however, allow you to make the mathematically correct play in each instance. When your chances of winning a particular hand are much greater than the dealer, the basic strategy play will usually have you putting more money on the table (by either doubling down or pair splitting). Sometimes basic strategy will turn a losing hand into a break even or even a winner by telling you to split. And just as important, basic strategy will minimize your losses in losing situations (remember those 12 through 17's!) by telling us which strategy decision over the long haul will allow us to lose less. There is no other way to becoming a winning blackjack player except learning the basic strategy. It is your first step to generate table profits so that you can "take the money and run."

4

Strategies for the Novice Player

This chapter contains a playing and money management strategy for the novice or beginning player. It does not involve card counting strategies which are part of the intermediate and advanced level strategies (Chapter 5 and 6).

Your playing strategy should follow the basic strategy discussed in the previous chapter with no deviations. Given a choice of single vs. multiple deck games, if possible select a single deck game with good rules (dealer stands on soft 17, no restrictions on double down). These games are readily available in Las Vegas and a two deck version in the Mississippi Gulf Coast casinos. In Atlantic City, your best game is the four deck game vs. six or eight decks.

How to Bet

For single and double deck games you need to scan the cards on the table to determine if there is an imbalance of high cards or low cards. For now, all you need to know is that the high value cards (10, J, Q, K, Ace) are player favorable cards and the small value cards (2, 3, 4, 5, 6) favor the dealer. Simply watch the cards on the table and make an estimation if the cards you see contain more high cards or low cards. For example, if you see these cards

$$10, 2, 5, 7, Ace, 3, 5, 6, 9$$

there are obviously more small cards (2, 5, 3, 5, 6) than high cards (10, Ace). Since there are more small cards than high cards on the table the opposite has to be true in the remaining cards to be dealt. When the remaining cards to be dealt are rich (or contain more) in high cards that is good for the player and you should bet more on the next hand. Likewise, if the remaining cards are rich in small cards, this is an unfavorable situation for the player and you should bet the minimum. You should continue to use the information of the cards that have been played to estimate the condition of the remaining cards (carry this information over from one round to the next). Thus if you see an excess of three high value cards vs. low cards after the first round, prior to the next deal you know the remaining cards contain an excess of three low value cards. On round two you scan the cards and estimate an excess of two high value cards vs. low. This information needs to be "added" to the information of the first round to determine the current status of the remaining cards (in this case, prior to round three the remaining cards contain five excess of low value cards vs. high). During the playout of a single deck, the condition of the remaining cards may change from neutral, to rich in high value cards, then possibly rich in low value cards depending upon how the cards fall on the table. Your goal is to watch the cards from round to round and track these imbalances of excess high or low value cards. Practice this estimation technique at home with a deck of cards. Simulate several player hands and then look at the cards to estimate if the remaining cards are neutral, rich in high cards, or rich in low cards. Check your estimation toward the end of the deck by turning the remaining cards over to see if in fact they agree with your estimate. You will be surprised with a little practice how well you can estimate the composition of cards left to be dealt.

Start your betting in the single or double deck game after the shuffle at 1 unit.[1] Then vary your bet size on subsequent rounds as follows:

If the deck is about neutral (equal balance of high and low value cards), then make your minimum bet (assume 1 unit).

Watch the aces! They are an important card for you because you get a bonus payoff on blackjacks (3 to 2). If you haven't seen any aces after a couple of rounds of play and the deck is still neutral, increase your bet to 2 units.

If the remaining cards in the deck in your estimation contain a disproportionate amount of small cards, either bet your minimum (1 unit) or more preferably, don't bet at all. Most casinos will allow you to do the latter (sit out a few hands).

If a lot of small cards appear on the first couple of rounds and you estimate the deck is now rich in high cards, increase your bet to 3 units. If you haven't seen any aces besides, then increase your bet to 4 units.

The following table summarizes the betting methodology just described.

Estimated Deck Composition	Bet Size
Rich in small cards	Sit out til deck becomes neutral or bet 1 unit
Neutral	1 unit
Neutral and no aces shown	2 units
Rich in high cards	3 units
Rich in high cards and no aces shown	4 units

---

[1]A betting unit as used in this book means the minimum basic unit bet. For example, a player who bets $5 as minimum, then $5 represents 1 unit.

The key to the above is to make your smallest bets when the deck is rich in small cards and only make your larger bets when the deck is rich in high cards.

When I first started playing blackjack seriously some 25 years ago, I used this very same betting methodology as a first step to becoming a winning player. Back then, single deck games were commonplace in Las Vegas and the majority of my visits were profitable. After a little practice and table experience, I found it easy to scan or track the cards to look for those imbalances of high or low cards in the remaining deck and adjust my bets accordingly. I have since taught thousands of beginning players this same, simple, playing and wagering strategy for single deck games. You won't win every hand or in fact every session, but over the long run you'll have a slight edge over the casino and will win more money than you lose.

This betting strategy can be used for two deck games although it is less effective than single deck games. It should *not* be used in 4, 6 or 8 deck games because the composition of the multiple decks does not change that much with the removal of a relatively small number of cards.

If you must play in a game that uses multiple decks, than I strongly urge you to learn either the intermediate or advanced strategies described in the next chapters. These strategies involve learning the technique of card counting. Trust me, it's not as difficult as it first appears. I have taught thousands of students in my gaming school how to card count and all of these students were just average players like you.

However, I am a realist and appreciate the fact that no matter what I (or anybody, for that matter) preaches about card counting, there are still those players who either won't or can't learn this technique. For their benefit and for the completeness of this book, I have included below a simple money management strategy for the non-card counter playing multiple decks. This strategy will <u>not</u> give the player a long term mathematical advantage in multiple deck games. However, for what it's worth, my wife has used this simple money management scheme every time she plays blackjack (over 20 years!) and overall she has won more than she has lost. Part of this is due to her skill at playing perfect basic strategy, a little bit of luck, and her strict adherence to the betting strategy that follows and the discipline to "take the money (profits) and run."

Money Management in Multiple Decks for Non-Card Counter

In this section, I will describe two methods of money management for the recreational blackjack player that is playing in a multiple deck game. This player is not a card counter but knows the basic strategy and wants to bet in a manner that will maximize his/her profits when the cards are going their way and lose as little as possible when they aren't.

The two optimum wagering techniques for this kind of player that I recommend are the use of winning progressions and proportional betting.

When you play blackjack you can make bets in any one of the following manner: always make the same bet; increase your bet when you feel you are going to win a hand; increase your bet based on previous wins or losses.

Technically speaking the safest way to bet in blackjack for a non-card counter is to always bet the same amount on every hand. The problem with this is that it isn't a very exciting way to gamble for most players. After all, most blackjack players are after a big win and in order to accomplish this, they must vary the size of the bet.

Increasing your bets based upon the feeling that you are due to win is foolish gambling. Unless you are card counting, you have no idea whether or not your chances of winning the next hand are good or bad. It is better to bet objectively based upon a predetermined pattern of bets (i.e. progressions) than bet subjectively based upon feelings.

Such predetermined betting is called betting progressions. You progress your bet to a higher level depending upon whether you won or lost the previous hand.

Let's eliminate once and for all those progressions that have you increase your bet size following a lose. These so called Martingale progressions are guaranteed to doom the player. So never increase your bet size following a loss in the hopes of catching up.

This leaves us with the following recommended money management scheme for the recreational player, namely the win progression. Here, bets are increased only after a hand is won. Once a losing hand occurs, the bet size is reduced to the minimum bet.

There are several win progressions that I can recommend. The simplest is a two level betting progression where the smaller bet is made following a loss and the larger bet is made following a win. For example, the small bet could be $5, the large bet, $10 or $15. Make your first bet $5, and if you win the hand, make your next bet $10, or $15. Continue to make your maximum bet until you lose. When a loss occurs, make your next bet $5.

The above method of betting was popularized by Charles Einstein in his book, "Basic Blackjack Betting."

A second win progression which I've used and taught for years is a simple 1, 2, 3, 5 back to 1 progression (this is the one my wife uses). For a $5 player, the betting levels are $5, 10, 15, and 25. Here a player starts with a $5 bet and progresses to the next bet level when a hand is won. As soon as a hand loses, the next bet is the basic $5 minimum bet. If the player is fortunate enough to win four hands in a row, I recommend that the profits be locked up and the progression restarted at the minimum $5 level.

If betting 5 units (or $25 for the $5 player) is too steep for your blood, then modify the progression to 1, 2, 3 back to 1. And for the very conservative player, I would suggest 1, 1, 2, 2 back to 1 (win two consecutive hands at 1 unit before you progress to 2 units). The point is to get in the habit of increasing your bets only following a win, never after a loss. And as soon as you lose a hand, revert back to the minimum one unit bet.

A suggested session bankroll for the above win progression is 20 times the minimum bet. To be safe, the player's total bankroll should be 100 times the minimum bet.

How does a win progression maximize wins and minimize losses? Suppose as an extreme case you sit down at the blackjack table and lose five hands in a row followed by a streak of five wins. If a player bets the same amount on every hand, he/she would be even. If instead the player uses the 1, 2, 3, 5 back to 1 progression with a minimum bet of $5, he/she would be behind $25 after the first 5 losses (5x$5) but when the streak of 5 wins occurs, would win $60 ($5+10+15+25+5). The $25 lost from the $60 won leaves a net win of $35 even though the player won as many hands as lost.

In technical terms, a win progression increases the variance a player can expect during any particular playing session. This means a player can win a lot more and likewise lose a lot more than the player who makes only the same bet size.

I showed you how a win progression generates more profits than straight one unit betting. Where the win progression falls apart is when hands are alternately winning and losing. If you used the 1-2-3-5 win progression and the sequence of winning and losing is W, L, W, L, W, L, the win progression will have you losing more than just straight one unit betting. Again, this is the risk you take in an attempt to maximize profits on streaks of wins of 3 hands or more.

A win progression has some scientific validity especially for multiple deck blackjack games. The favorability or unfavorability of a particular shoe is predetermined based upon the nature of the cards situated behind the cut card (i.e. the unplayed cards). If these cards which are not put into play are rich in ten value cards, then the probability of consecutive dealer wins increases for this shoe. Likewise, if the mix of cards situated behind the cut card contain many low value cards, then the probability of your experiencing win streaks increases. Thus when the shoe favors the dealer, you will be losing the minimum bet on dealer streaks of wins. However, during a favorable shoe you will experience more win streaks and consequently will be making larger bets.

Your average bet will be somewhat larger in a favorable shoe compared to an unfavorable shoe. And this is what allows you to win more in winning streaks and lose less in losing streaks.

Keep in mind that if the dealer gets 19's and 20's on every hand, you'll end up a loser no matter what kind of betting scheme you use. But in the long run, you'll fare better with a simple win progression and the discipline to quit when you are ahead (take the money and run!!).

Always be satisfied with modest profits because in the long term they will add up to sizeable profits which will more than balance the occasional losing sessions.

The technique of proportional betting is an alternate betting strategy for the recreational player. First the player must size his/her bankroll equal to 100 times his/her minimum bet. If you are a $5 minimum bet player, you need at least a $500 bankroll. A $3 minimum bet player requires a $300 bankroll.

With the proper bankroll to minimum bet ratio (100 to 1), you now play perfect basic strategy and always make the same size bet. In other words, for a $500 bankroll, every bet you make during the first shoe should be $5. Naturally, on some hands you might have to add another $5 bet on double-downs and pair splits, but your initial bet should remain at $5 for the entire shoe.

At the completion of the shoe, add up your chips to determine the status of your bankroll. Divide the amount of your bankroll by 100 and this will give you the bet size for the second shoe.

For example, if your bankroll was $600 after the first shoe, (you won $100 in the first shoe) your standard bet size for the second shoe should be $6.00 (not $5.00).

In the event you lost $100 during the first shoe and your new bankroll stands at $400, your bet size for shoe number 2 should drop from $5 to $4.

By always making bets in proportion to your bankroll at any time (or during each shoe), you will naturally be betting more when you are winning in a favorable shoe and less when losing in an unfavorable shoe. In the event of a long series of losing shoes, this method of betting will keep you in the game a lot longer than any other method of betting. The more staying power you have, the greater is the likelihood that you will be able to recoup some of your losses if and when the cards turn in your favor.

In most casinos, the minimum bet on the blackjack tables is $3 (or more likely $5). This means you must have at least $300 or $500 bankroll to be properly bankrolled to bet in this manner. If you can only afford a $100 bankroll and you are making $2 or $3 bets, you are overbetting in relation to your bankroll. This means that you have increased the probability of losing your $100 bankroll simply due to the normal fluctuations inherent in the game of blackjack.

It is not necessary, of course, to convert your entire bankroll into chips at the table. You may only convert part of it and this part becomes your session bankroll (keep the rest in your pocket or purse or even at home). But for the purposes of determining the status of your bankroll, use the entire bankroll as a base.

A player who uses proportional betting should be satisfied with a modest win. In the event you can do no wrong at the tables and your winnings keep increasing, by all means keep playing and try to win as much as you can. But when the tide turns, and you begin to lose back some of your profits, be prepared to take the money (profits) and run.

Although I present the above betting progressions as an alternate to bet sizing based upon deck composition, I again strongly urge even the recreational player to learn how to keep track of the cards as they are played and use this information for betting adjustments. Over the short term it's possible to win with the betting progressions but your goal is to play for the long run. Make the commitment to learn basic strategy and then either play in single deck games using the deck composition for bet adjustments or in multiple deck games, learn the intermediate or advanced card counting techniques discussed in chapters 5 and 6.

Summary

Your first step to become a winning blackjack player if you are a novice or beginner is to do the following:

1. Learn the basic blackjack playing strategy. Do not deviate from this strategy.
2. Play in single deck games with favorable rules (ideally dealer stands on soft 17, no restrictions on doubling, multiple pair splits allowed). If the casino offers these rules plus doubling after pair splitting, you'll actually have the edge just with basic strategy.
3. If single deck games are not available, play in double deck games vs. 4, 6 or 8 deck games.
4. Determine the deck composition by watching the cards as they are played. Increase your bets when the deck is rich in high value cards, decrease your bet when rich in low cards (or better yet, sit out a few hands).
5. Be satisfied with modest profits. If you are able to generate profits equal to 20% or more of your starting bankroll, be ready to "take the money and run" when the tide turns. REMEMBER THAT THE NAME OF THE GAME IS TO WIN MONEY. DON'T EVER LOSE YOUR TABLE PROFITS BACK TO THE CASINO!!

5

Intermediate Blackjack Strategies
The Streak/Count System

The intermediate blackjack strategy discussed in this chapter centers around learning a simple plus minus card counting system. This is not as difficult as it first appears. In fact I have taught thousands of average players in my schools and seminars the technique of card counting. Take a positive approach that you can and will learn it and I guarantee you will be rewarded with many profitable blackjack sessions.

Before I get into the discussion of card counting, I want to digress and summarize the history of winning blackjack strategies and give credit to the individuals who have made major contributions to our understanding of blackjack.

It all started in 1953 when Roger Baldwin and co-workers undertook the first scientific analysis of the game of blackjack. Using hand calculators, they were able to develop the first basic blackjack playing strategy which they published in the *Journal of the American Statistical Association* in 1956. Baldwin and his co-workers then published a book, *Playing Blackjack to Win* in 1956.

In the early 1960s, Dr. Edward Thorp used high speed computers to develop the first card counting system for blackjack. He published his ten count system in the classic book, *Beat the Dealer* (1962), which became a best seller. His message was quite clear. Blackjack is a game of skill, not just luck, and the skillful player can beat the casinos.

The casinos in Las Vegas began to panic after Thorp's revelation. They started to change the rules of blackjack but in the process upset the majority of blackjack players who had no clue as to how to win. Although it was theoretically possible to have the edge over the casinos with Thorp's card counting system, it was extremely difficult to implement for the average person in actual casino play. Therefore, blackjack popularity grew tremendously because of this discovery that it was a "beatable game." Ironically, the casino's profits also increased because more and more players flocked to play the "beatable game" but did not possess the skills or knowledge to do it.

The next blackjack guru that came on the scene was Lawrence Revere (1970's). His book, *Playing Blackjack as a Business*, simplified card counting systems and also presented the basic strategy in colored charts to make learning the strategy even easier. Revere's book started me on a career of doing my own studies about the games.

Julian Braun, who worked for IBM and collaborated with Revere, further refined the basic strategy and the high-low count developed earlier by Harvey Dubner (1963). His book, *How to Play Winning Blackjack*, clearly explained the mathematics of the basic strategy charts. I found Julian's book to be extremely helpful to explain the reasons for certain basic strategy plays to novice players. Unfortunately, the book is now out of print.

Other authors and researchers came onto the scene in the 70's and 80's. Stanford Wong, a professional blackjack player, wrote the classic book, *Professional Blackjack*. This was and still is the bible for card counters. I've learned a tremendous amount about blackjack through the writings of Stanford Wong (he still authors books and a newsletter). The late Ken Uston popularized the concept of card counting teams in his book, *Million Dollar Blackjack*. Ian Anderson gave us new techniques for disguising our card counting skills in his book, *Turning the Tables on Las Vegas*. Stanley Roberts started one of the first schools to teach players how to count. He was also one of the first to publish a national gambling magazine, *Gambling Times*, devoted to gambling.

Other major contributors to our knowledge of blackjack during this era included: Peter Griffin (detailed mathematical studies and book, *The Theory of Blackjack*), Carlon Chambliss and Thomas Roginski (*Fundamentals of Blackjack*, a very thorough survey of the entire field of blackjack), Arnold Snyder (monthly blackjack publication, *Blackjack Forum*), Lance Humble and Carl Cooper (*World's Greatest Blackjack Book*, detailed study of his card counting system), Jerry Patterson (*Blackjack - A Winner's Handbook and New Studies into Target Blackjack Systems*), Steve Forte (*Read the Dealer*, which explains how to read dealer tells), Michael Dalton (*Blackjack. A Professional Reference*, the first comprehensive reference book on the game), Bryce Carlson (*Blackjack for Blood*, a professional player's book on how to win), Bill Zender (a casino supervisor who wrote *Card Counting for the Casino Executive*) and Donald Schlesinger (a regular contributor to *Blackjack Forum* and an excellent blackjack mathematician).

There certainly were other contributors but the above were the ones who made the greatest impact on my knowledge of the game of blackjack. I publicly thank them.

As mentioned earlier, in order to be a consistent winning blackjack player you must learn the techniques of card counting. Let's get started by first understanding the theory behind counting the cards.

Blackjack Card Counting

There isn't a day that goes by without someone asking me about blackjack card counting. What is it? Does it work? Can you do it with six decks? How much can I win? In this section, we'll sort out all the mysteries of card counting and show you it's really not all that complicated.

In the game of blackjack, your probability of winning a particular hand is very dependent upon the mix of the cards remaining to be played. If this mix of cards happens to contain an abundance of high value cards (ex. 10's), then your chances of winning increases. On the other hand, if the mix contains an abundance of low cards (ex. 2 through 6), then your chances of winning are not good. This has been proven over and over again by countless millions of computer studies, i.e. a deck (or shoe) rich in tens will favor the player and a deck deficient in tens or containing an excess of low cards will favor the dealer.

The reasons why a ten rich deck favors the player is because, 1) there will be more blackjack and pat hands (17 through 21) dealt. Even though the dealer has an equal chance of receiving a good hand from a ten rich deck, the dealer doesn't get paid 3 to 2 on a blackjack hand (but you will!). 2) With a two card hand totaling 9, 10, 11, the dealer can't double in a ten rich deck, but you can. 3) The dealer's chances of busting a 12 through 16 hand is greater in a ten rich deck. Remember you don't have to hit these hands if you don't want to; the dealer however must. So you see there are many advantages and options available for the player to increase his winnings in a ten rich deck whereas the dealer doesn't have these advantages.

Now a deck deficient in tens or containing a surplus of low cards, favors the dealer because the chances of him receiving a pat hand (17 through 21) are good when he must (by the rules) hit his 12 through 16 hands.

If you don't believe all this try this test at home. Play several hundred hands of blackjack with a deck of cards in which you've removed the 5's and 6's (and created a ten rich deck). Repeat the process, only this time remove the tens and jacks (now you have a ten poor deck). You will find you should win more playing with the ten rich deck.

Now in order to know when a deck is ten rich or ten poor, you must keep track of all the cards as they are played. If you obviously see a lot of little cards being played then it stands to reason that there is probably a lot of high cards left in the remaining deck which signifies a ten rich deck and your chances of winning increases. If this is the case, a card counter, or a person who is keeping track of these cards, would increase his bet. On the other hand, if the counter knows from "counting" the cards that the remaining cards to be played are ten poor, he would bet the minimum since his chances of winning are not good.

This illustrative example of how card counting works should help you to understand this concept.

In a single deck of cards there are 26 red cards (hearts and diamonds) and 26 black cards (clubs and spades). Assume we played a game whereby you can bet as much as you'd like, that a card selected at random from the 52 card deck will be the color you preselect. It should be obvious that your chances of selecting a red card or black card is 50:50 since there is an even distribution of red (26) and black (26) cards. Let's assume you bet 1 chip on a red card and you then proceed to pick a red card from the deck. You have won 1 chip. Now we play the game again by reshuffling the remaining 51 cards. How much would you bet and on what color? You should be betting on black. Why? Because by seeing the previous card selected (red) you now have the knowledge that in the remaining 51 cards, there are 26 black and only 25 red. There is one more black card than red, so the chances of selecting black are slightly greater than those of selecting red. Of course, there are no guarantees that you will select a black card, but still, this is the best percentage play for you to make.

Of course, in actual casino play you won't be counting red or black cards. In fact the card counting method which I've used and taught successfully for years is what is known as a simple plus minus count and it goes like this. Every time you see a 2, 3, 4, 5 or 6 card you assign them a count value of +1. The 10, J, Q, K, Ace count −1. The 7, 8, 9 are neutral and count as 0.

Count Value of Cards

2, 3, 4, 5, 6	count +1
7, 8, 9	count 0
10, J, Q, K, A	count - 1

At the start of a shoe, your count is 0 and as each card is played you must arithmetically add its count value. For example, if you see the following cards played: Ace, 6, 4, 3, 9 - you would count −1 (the ace) plus + 1 (the 6) plus +1 (the 4) plus +1 (the 3) plus 0 (the 9) and your arithmetic total or count is +2. You continue to count (or add) all the cards until a round is completed and you have a final count. If this count is a positive number you generally have a deck which is favorable because more high cards remain in the deck (in order to get a positive count you must have counted a lot of little cards). If instead the count is negative, more tens, picture cards and aces have been played and the advantage shifts to the casino. A counter now enjoys the ideal playing conditions. If the count is positive, his/her chances of winning increase and therefore bets larger amounts. If the count is negative, the counter bets the minimum or nothing at all (why bet when the dealer's chances of winning are greater than yours?) Thus over the long run, card counters lose as little as possible when their chances of winning are poor but more importantly, they win much more when they have the advantage. In fact a counter has up to a 1 to 2% advantage over the casino, something which is impossible to do in any other casino game.

Obviously this technique is not something you learn overnight. If it were that easy, everyone would learn it and the game of blackjack as we know it would cease. However, anyone with average intelligence and with proper training can learn these skills and join a select minority of casino gamers that possess the skills to win more than they lose.

Learning How to Count

The best way to learn how to count cards is to practice a little each day. You'll be surprised how quickly you'll be able to master card counting by following the plan outlined below.

First you must be able to recognize the card count values. Practice this by taking a deck of cards and flipping them over one at a time while calling out the count value of each card. For example if the first card is a six of diamonds, you would call out "plus one." If the next card were an ace of spades, you'd call out "minus one."

Keep going through a deck of cards until you are able to rapidly recognize that all the 2, 3, 4, 5, 6's count plus one, the 7, 8, 9 count zero and the 10's, picture cards and aces count minus one. Keep practicing until you've memorized the count value for each card.

After you've mastered recognizing the count value for every card, you must now learn how to keep the running count or arithmetic sum of all the pluses and minus cards. To do this, take your deck of cards and flip them over one card at a time. Add (or subtract) each count value to the preceding count to determine the running count. For example, suppose the first card were a two. Your count is plus one.

Card	Count Value	Running Count
two	plus one	plus one

The next card is a four. This card has a count value of plus one. You now arithmetically add the plus one to the previous count (plus one) to arrive at the new running count (plus two).

Card	Count Value	Running Count
two	plus one	plus one
four	plus one	plus two

The next card is a six. It's count value is also plus one. Therefore you're running count status is plus three.

Card	Count Value	Running Count
two	plus one	plus one
four	plus one	plus two
six	plus one	plus three

The next card is a seven. It's count value is zero, therefore the running count remains plus three.

Card	Count Value	Running Count
two	plus one	plus one
four	plus one	plus two
six	plus one	plus three
seven	zero	plus three

Next is a queen. It has a count value of minus one. When you arithmetically add a minus one to the previous running count of plus three you arrive at the new running count of plus two (i.e. $+3 - 1 = +2$).

Card	Count Value	Running Count
two	plus one	plus one
four	plus one	plus two
six	plus one	plus three
seven	zero	plus three
queen	minus one	plus two

Continue this exercise of flipping over one card at a time while keeping the running count. If you do this exercise accurately, at the end of a 52 card deck your running count should be zero. This is because the plus minus count that you are learning is a balanced count. There are just as many plus cards (20) as there are minus cards (20) in a 52 deck of cards resulting in all cards canceling and a final sum (or running count) of zero.

Keep practicing this exercise until you develop the accuracy to end up with a zero count at least 8 out of 10 times. Don't worry about speed. For now, it's important to learn accuracy.

Where most players have difficulty is with negative numbers. If your running count is minus two and the next card is an ace (count value of minus one), your new running count is minus three. In other words, adding a negative number to a negative number gives a larger negative number (minus two plus minus one yields minus three).

The following diagram can be used to help remember this fact.

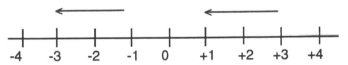

If I add a minus two to a plus three my new sum is plus one. If instead I add a minus one to a minus two, my new sum is minus 3.

After you've mastered counting down a deck of cards with 80% accuracy, repeat the process using two decks. Your goal is now 90% accuracy (9 out of 10 times you count down two decks of cards you should end up with a zero count).

Once you've developed accuracy, you now have to work on speed. To be a successful card counter in the fast pace casino environment, you must count down a deck of cards in less than 30 seconds with 90% accuracy. Keep practicing the running count with your deck of cards until you develop speed and accuracy.

In actual casino play, it's not necessary to count every card if you learn the technique of cancellation. Thus if I observe the cards of a player who shows a four and a ten (and stands on 14), I don't have to worry about adding the count values of these cards to my running count because the two cards cancel (the four with a count value of plus one cancels the ten with a count value of minus one). In other words a plus card will cancel a minus card to give the sum of zero.

Learning to cancel plus and minus cards is a tremendous help when card counting. To learn this, take your deck of cards and flip over two, three or four cards at a time on a table. Scan the cards and if you see a plus and a minus value card, ignore them. Keep turning over two or move cards while keeping the running count and cancelling the high cards (minus cards) with the low cards (plus cards).

If you practice card counting using the above suggestions you will be able to accurately count a deck of cards quicker than you think. And once you've practiced and learned this skill, it is something you'll be able to use every time you play blackjack for the rest of your life.

But let's talk a minute about how to count the cards in actual casino play. Here you'll have to contend with seeing and counting other player cards, the dealer's cards and your cards to keep an accurate count. The best way to tell you how to count the cards during actual playing conditions is to describe to you how I do it.

I always try to sit at the anchor or third base side of the table so I can count all the player cards (in face up games) before I act on my hand. After all players receive their initial two cards face up, I start the count for this round by first counting the dealer's upcard, then focusing on the cards of the first base player. I don't count every card. I use the technique of cancellation as I observe the two (or more) cards for the first base player. By using cancellation, I don't have to do as much mental arithmetic to keep the count. I then go to the next player's hand and do the same. I can usually count each player's hand as they in turn give their signal to the dealer (hit, stand, etc.). The worst scenario is when the dealer shows a small card and all players rapidly give a signal that they want to stand. Believe it or not, this doesn't happen to often because usually several players don't know any better and will procrastinate a few seconds before they invariably draw a card (thanks to them, it makes counting the cards a lot easier for me!). In the event you haven't been able to count all the player cards before the dealer points to you for a playing decision, don't fret. Just remember where you left off counting the cards, play out your hand, then go back and pick up the count.

The final cards to count are your cards, the dealer's downcard and his/her draw cards.

In single or double deck games where player cards are dealt face down, here is how I handle counting the cards. I count my initial two cards, then the dealer's upcard, all the players' draw cards and down cards when players bust. Finally I count my draw cards, the dealer's down card, any of his/her draw cards, and then all players' downcards as the dealer flips them over to determine each player's hand total.

There are obviously other ways to count the cards on the table as the cards are played. The important point is you want to be able to keep an accurate count because if you err it could wipe out your advantage. And from my experience, I can keep a much more accurate count if I count the cards in the same sequence every time.

Practice this by dealing yourself several hands at home to simulate a game with two or more players. Better yet, have a spouse or friend act as dealer while you practice counting the cards as they are dealt. When you think you've mastered this, go to a casino and try to keep the count of a game in progress as a spectator. Be certain you can keep an accurate count under casino conditions before you actually start playing.

Effect of Card Removal

Peter Griffin in his book, *The Theory of Blackjack*, describes the effects on the casino's advantage in blackjack when each card is removed from a deck of 52 cards. The data below shows the effects of removal in percentages for every card (positive percentage is a player advantage; negative percent is a player disadvantage).

Card	Effect of Removal (in percent)
2	+0.38
3	+0.44
4	+0.55
5	+0.69
6	+0.46
7	+0.28
8	0
9	−0.18
10	−0.51
Ace	−0.61

As the chart shows, certain cards have different effects on the casino advantage when removed. A removal of a single 5 from the deck would give the player an advantage of +0.7% while the removal of a single ten would put him at a −0.5% disadvantage. The above information on card removal is in fact what is used to develop the simple plus minus count. Notice the cards from 2 through 6 have positive effects when removed. Therefore we group those as low cards in our count and give each card value a plus one for counting purposes. Similarly, the 10's and aces have large negative card removal effects and therefore are assigned the count value of minus one. The eight has no effect on card removal, and the 7 and 9 very little effect. We therefore group these as neutral cards for card counting purposes and give them the count value of zero.

What Should the Count Tell Us

Any counting system needs to provide us information on:

when to bet more and
when to deviate from basic strategy

You can calculate how efficient a card counting system is with respect to the above. The plus minus count recommended in this book has a betting efficiency of 0.97 and playing efficiency of 0.51. What this means is that the simple plus minus count is very efficient at detecting those situations in which we have the advantage and should be increasing our bet. The playing efficiency is not nearly as efficient to detect situations in which we should vary our basic playing strategy. However, the system is easy to use and will give us enough information to give us the overall advantage over the casino.

Streak Count System

This is a simple system that a first time card counter can use to vary the bet size based upon the count. It combines the win progression betting with the count for bet size variation.

The system is quite simple.

1. Always use the basic playing strategy learned in Chapter 3 for playing decisions.
2. Never take insurance.
3. Use the streak count betting system explained below to vary the size of the bet.

The streak count betting system for blackjack is a unique betting strategy incorporating the plus minus count. It was developed by my associate Dick Ramm and I. It combines aspects of a win progression and qualitative bet sizing based upon the running count. The betting is simple and easy for the beginning card counter to master.

There are five levels of bets in the progression with the first level representing the minimum 1 unit bet and the fifth level, the maximum 7 unit bet. Note the 1 to 7 unit bet spread.

Level	1	2	3	4	5
Units	1	2	3	5	7

The concept of this betting system is that when the remaining cards become unfavorable for the player, we use the same win betting progression discussed in chapter 4, namely 1, 2, 3, 5 back to 1. But when the remaining cards turn favorable for us, we shift to a more aggressive betting progression of 2, 3, 5, 7 and staying at 7 until a loss occurs. In other words, the system will automatically have you betting more in favorable situations and less in unfavorable situations.

To implement this betting system, first determine when the cards turn favorable for us using the chart below. Any running count higher than the numbers in the right column means the cards are favorable for us.

Game	Favorable
1 or 2 decks	+1 or more
4 and 6 decks	+3 or more
8 decks	+5 or more

Any running count lower than the numbers in the right column means the cards are unfavorable for us.

After determining the favorability of the cards follow these rules to adjust your bets:

1. Progress your bet from level 1 to 4 following a win regardless of whether the running count is favorable or unfavorable. The only exception to this rule is if the running count is -5 or more

negative in 4, 6, 8 deck games or -2 or more negative in single and double deck games. When this occurs, this necessitates an immediate adjustment of the bet to level 1 (1 unit).

2. If you win at level 4 (5 units) and the running count is unfavorable, bet 1 unit.

3. If you win at level 4 (5 units) and the running count is favorable, proceed to level 5 (7 unit maximum bet).

4. Whenever you lose at any level and the running count is unfavorable, bet 1 unit.

5. Whenever you lose at any level and the running count is favorable, bet 2 units (level 2).

6. If you win at level 5 (7 unit maximum bet) and the running count is favorable, continue to bet 7 units. Whenever the running count turns unfavorable, (following a win or loss) bet 1 unit.

7. If a hand ties (push) stay at the same bet level. The only exception is if a hand ties at level 5 (7 unit maximum bet) and the running count is unfavorable. In this case, bet 1 unit.

8. If a hand is split, the net result of the split hands determines whether you've won, lost or tied the hand.

Some important conclusions that may be derived from these rules are the following:

1. Your minimum bet made in a favorable shoe will always be 2 units (level 2).

2. The 1 unit bet is only made if the remaining cards are unfavorable and a) you lost your last bet, b) you won at level 4 or 5, or c) the running count is −5 or worse (4, 6, 8 decks) or −2 or worse for single and double deck games.

3. The only way to make the large 7 unit bet is to have won the level 4 (5 unit) bet and have a favorable situation. In fact you must have a

favorable situation in order to wager the maximum 7 units.

4. Once you wager 7 units (level 5), you will continue to do so as long as you continue to win and
the game is favorable. If either of these conditions changes, the bet size is reduced.

The following table can be used as a study aid to
learn this betting system. The left hand column of numbers
represents the bet size (in units). The numbers in the table
indicate what the next bet should be depending upon
whether the hand won or lost and whether or not the game
is favorable (F) or unfavorable (U).

BET SIZE INDICATOR (in units)

LAST BET MADE	WON		LOST	
	F	U	F	U
1	2	2	2	1
2	3	3	2	1
3	5	5	2	1
5	7	1	2	1
7	7	1	2	1

F = Favorable   U = Unfavorable

For example, if you wager 3 units and you win the
hand and the running count indicates a favorable situation,
your next bet is 5 units. Likewise, if you wager 5 units, lose
the hand and have an unfavorable situation, the next bet
you should make is 1 unit. The above betting methodology
will automatically have you making larger bets in favorable

situations and smaller bets in unfavorable situations.

It is designed also to take advantage of your win streaks (which have a higher probability of occurring in favorable situations) but can still occur as well in unfavorable situations. Since large bets are only made with profits from winning succeeding hands in the progression, this betting methodology minimizes your chances of going broke by losing too many large bets in succession. And most importantly, this method of betting automatically disguises the fact that you are a skillful card counter (you'll never be increasing your bet size by more than 2 units at a time).

With the above betting strategy, your session bankroll should be equal to 30 times the basic 1 unit bet. Your total bankroll should be 4 times the session bankroll.

Quit a session if you've either lost your session bankroll or you've managed to win 10 to 20% of your session bankroll. If you are winning like crazy (which will happen from time to time!), keep playing but be sure you quit with your profits when you start to lose. I'll have more to say about this in Chapter 9.

The following statistics about the above betting strategy might interest you.

1. In general you will average about 150 hands per session (about a 2 hour playing session).
2. Your average bet size using the bet progression, as determined from computer studies, is 3.0 units per hand. With a total bankroll of 120 units, this represents an average bet to stake ratio of 1 to 40.
3. Assuming 3.0 units per hand x 150 hands per session, this equals a total of 450 units risked per session. It would take a casino edge of at least 6.6% to grind out your 30 unit session bankroll (6.6% of 450 equals 30).
4. This course of play will take 9 or 10 consecutive sessions, in each of which you lose your entire 30

unit session bankroll to wipe out your 120 unit
stake. This is the worst that can happen.

The streak count betting system when incorporated
with the basic playing strategy will give you a slight edge
(about 0.5%) over the casino. To further increase your edge
you must learn the technique of true count wagering and
strategy deviation discussed in the next chapter.

6

Advanced Level Blackjack Strategies

In the previous chapter, bet sizing was based upon the knowledge of the running count. All running counts equal to or greater than a specific positive running count were considered to be a favorable situation to the player. In doing this, the betting system avoided taking into consideration the absolute value of the running count when varying the bet size. In essence, we used the concept of qualitative bet adjustments to simplify the strategy; namely, no matter how large or small your advantage, the bet size was advanced the same using the recommended bet progression.

To be mathematically accurate in adjusting the bet size according to the count, which is very important for multiple deck games, it is necessary to use quantitative betting, or betting in proportion to the absolute value of the count. Thus, the higher the plus count, the greater your advantage and the greater should be the size of your bet.

Removing one ten value card from one full deck will have the same effect as removing four tens from a four deck shoe or six tens from a six deck shoe. Thus, a running count of +6 at the beginning of a six deck shoe is not nearly as favorable as a +6 running count in the middle of a shoe.

So, in order to accomplish quantitative bet sizing, it in necessary to adjust the running count for the number of decks left in the shoe to get a normalized or adjusted running count per deck. The latter is called the true count.

The calculation of the true count is also required to determine when to deviate from basic strategy under certain deck composition.

To compute the true count at any point during a blackjack game, you must divide the running count by the number of unplayed decks of cards. Sounds difficult, but as you'll soon see it's a technique that can be readily learned.

The equation that relates the running count to the true count is as follows:

$$True\ Count = \frac{Running\ Count}{No.\ of\ Decks\ Unplayed}$$

For example, a running count of +6 into the first deck of a new shoe (6 deck game) translates to a true count of +1.

$$True\ Count = \frac{+6}{6} = +1$$

Suppose the running count was +2 and two decks remained unplayed of a four deck game. The true count would be +2 (running count) divided by 2 (number of unplayed decks of cards) or +1.

$$True\ Count = \frac{+2}{2} = +1$$

Negative running counts yield negative true counts. Suppose the running count was −4 and two decks remain in a six deck game. The true count is −2.

$$True\ Count = \frac{-4}{2} = -2$$

If your conversion of running count to true count yields a fraction, I recommend you round up for fractions greater than one half, and round down for fractions equal to or less than one half.[1] For example, if your running count is +3 and two decks remain in a four deck game, you should estimate your true count at +1.

$$True\ Count = \frac{+3}{2} = +1.5\ or\ +1$$

Suppose your running count is +5 and three decks are left (6 deck game). Your true count is +2.

$$True\ Count = \frac{+5}{3} = +1.66\ or\ +2$$

Let's review how you determine the number of unplayed decks of cards left to be played (the denominator in the true count equation).

First you need to know how many decks of cards the casino is using at their blackjack tables. You should know this even before you start to play, but if you're not sure simply ask the dealer or floor person (after a while you'll be able to easily recognize by the number of cards in the shoe or discard tray prior to the shuffle whether it's a four, six or eight deck game).

Let's assume it's a six deck game. As play progresses, the dealer will remove all the played cards on the table and place them in a stack in the discard tray (set to the dealer's right). This stack of cards is what you focus on. You eyeball

---

[1]This is OK to do when using the true count to vary bet size. However, for strategy variation, we will not be rounding.

the stack and estimate how many decks of cards have been played. Let's assume you estimate about two decks of cards stacked in the discard tray. To determine the number of unplayed decks (the denominator in the true count equation) you simply subtract in your head the number of decks you see in the discard tray from the total number of decks being used at the table. In our example, it's a six deck shoe game, you estimate two decks in the discard tray, therefore the number of unplayed decks left in the shoe is six minus two or four. The latter is what you would use to divide into the running count to compute the true count.

Let's try a few examples. The first column in the table below indicates the number of decks in the discard tray. The second column is the total number of decks being used at the table. The third column lists your running count and the last column is the calculated true count. Make sure you can follow the logic as to how the true count was computed from the running count in the examples below.

# Decks in Discard Tray	# Decks in Game	Running Count	True Count
2	4	+6	+3
1	4	+3	+1
3	6	+4	+1
2	4	−2	−1
4	6	+8	+4

In my earlier days of playing blackjack, I purchased an inexpensive discard tray from a casino supply house and stacked different decks of cards in the tray to get a feel of what two, three, four, etc. stack of cards looked like. With a little practice you'd be amazed at how quickly and accurately you can estimate the number of decks stacked in the tray.

What if you glance at the discard tray and estimate what appears to be about 2½ decks of cards. The table is using four decks of cards. In this situation, you first estimate the number of unplayed decks by subtracting 2½ from 4 (answer is 1½). You then divide the running count (+2) by the number of unplayed decks (1½ or 3/2). When dealing with fractions, it's a lot easier to multiply by the inverse of the fraction than to divide by the fractions. Therefore to calculate the true count multiply +2 by 2/3. The true count is +1⅓ or simply +1.

$$True\ Count = \frac{+2}{3/2} \ or \ +2 \times \frac{2}{3} = 1\tfrac{1}{3}\ or\ +1$$

If dividing (or multiplying) by fractions is not your cup of tea, than just do the best job you can to estimate the number of decks in the discard tray to the nearest whole number. If you glance at the discard tray and estimate what appears to be 2½ decks, be conservative and round down to 2. By rounding down you'll be calculating a true count that will be slightly less than the actual true count.

Now let's discuss the situation of playing in a single or two deck hand held game. In two deck games, you'll need to estimate the number of decks in the discard tray to the nearest half deck and in single deck games, to the nearest third. Let's review these situations in more detail.

Single Deck

Some casinos use a discard tray in single deck games and others do not. If one isn't used, the discards are placed face up under the remaining cards by the dealer. I'll address both situations.

Whenever multiple decks of cards are used, the true count is most always less than the running count. In the case of a single deck, the opposite occurs for the most part, namely, the true count will be higher than the running count. The reason is that for a single deck game, you need to calculate the true count after one-third, one-half, and two-thirds of the cards have been dealt (you will always be dividing by a number less than one which is why the true count will be greater than the running count once play begins).

The following table is an easy way to remember how to compute the true count in single deck games that use a discard tray.

# Cards in Discard Tray	Fraction of Deck Unplayed	Multiplier for True Count
approx. 17 or 1/3 deck	2/3	3/2
approx. 26 or 1/2 deck	1/2	2
approx. 35 or 2/3 deck	1/3	3

Let's try some examples to see how easy it really is. Suppose your running count is +2, you glance at the discard tray and estimate one half deck of cards. That means there are still one half deck left to be played. You convert your running count to true count by multiplying by 2. The true count in this situation is +4.

$$True\ Count = \frac{Running\ Count}{Fraction\ of\ deck\ unplayed}$$

$$= \frac{+2}{\frac{1}{2}}\ or\ +2\ x\ 2\ =\ +4$$

Before you play in single deck games, take a deck of cards and group them into piles of 17, 26 and 35 to get a feel for what that many cards stacked looks like. Remember you only have a few seconds to glance at the discard tray to determine how many fraction of a deck of cards are stacked. That one glance will give you the information you need to determine the multiplier for converting running count to true count.

Here are several examples for practice:

Fraction of Deck in Discard Tray	Multiplier	Running Count	True Count
1/3	3/2	+2	+3
1/2	2	−1	−2
2/3	3	+2	+6
2/3	3	−2	−6
1/3	3/2	+3	+4

An alternate technique can be used to determine the multiplier for running to true count conversion. This is in fact the way to do this conversion when the dealer places the discards under the remaining cards. This technique is based on learning a multiplier for each round of hands dealt in a single deck game.

As a general rule, on average 2.7 cards are played per hand. Therefore, if you play head up with the dealer (just you and the dealer - no other players), 5.4 cards are used on average per round. Likewise, we can use this information to calculate how many cards would be used per round as a function of number of players. Based on this we can also compute a multiplier from running count to true count.

When playing single deck games, you should try to play head up as much as possible. Never play with more than two other players at the table. Therefore the following table lists the calculated number of hands dealt per round for one, two and three player games, and the calculated running count to true count multiplier.

ONE PLAYER

# Rounds Played	# Cards Played	Multiplier
1	5	1
2	11	1
3	16	3/2
4	22	3/2
5	27	2
6	32	3
7	39	4

TWO PLAYERS

# Rounds Played	# Cards Played	Multiplier
1	8	1
2	16	3/2
3	24	2
4	32	3
5	41	5

THREE PLAYERS

# Rounds Played	# Cards Played	Multiplier
1	11	1
2	22	3/2
3	32	3
4	43	5

In some cases, I've rounded the multiplier to avoid wild fractions (remember we need a method to estimate true count that is fairly accurate but just as important, easy to do at the tables).

To use this information, all you need do is memorize the corresponding multiplier for the number of rounds played and then use the multiplier to convert your running count to true count.

For example, suppose I was playing a single deck head up game. My running count and true count is estimated to be the same for the first two rounds of play (multiplier is 1). After the third and fourth round of play, I convert my running count to true count by multiplying by 3/2. On the final rounds of play, my multiplier increases by one for each round (2 then 3 then 4).

When I first started to use this technique I wrote down the multiplier and corresponding # rounds played on the back of a hand held basic strategy card. The latter was (and still is) tolerated and when I referred to it to remember the multiplier, it also gave the impression I was a novice player checking my basic strategy. I kept track of the number of rounds played with my chips. After every round I placed one of my chips in a separate stack. All I had to do was to count the number of chips in my "special stack" to determine the round.

You will soon see that for single (and double) deck games we will use only the running count for sizing our bets and compute the true count for only seventeen specific playing situations. This simplification makes it a lot easier to remember how to bet and when to deviate from basic strategy.

Double Deck Games

Discard trays are universally used in double deck games. We'll estimate the number of cards in the discard tray to the nearest one third or one half deck to compute our multiplier for running count to true count.

#Decks in Discard Tray	# Decks Left Unplayed	Multiplier for True Count
1/3	1 2/3 or 5/3	3/5
1/2	1 1/2 or 3/2	2/3
2/3	1 1/3 or 4/3	3/4
1	1	1
1 1/3	2/3	3/2
1 1/2	1/2	2
1 2/3	1/3	3

Let's try another example. Your running count is +4, you glance at the discard tray and estimate 2/3 deck of cards. Your multiplier to convert running count to true count is 3/4. Therefore, your true count is three fourths of +4 or +3.

$$True\ Count = \frac{Running\ Count}{\#\ of\ Decks\ unplayed}$$

$$= \frac{+4}{1\frac{1}{3}}\ or\ +4\ x\ \frac{3}{4} = +3$$

Let's summarize the conversion of running count to true count.

1. You convert the running count to true count in multiple deck games prior to making a bet and for determining when to deviate from the basic playing strategy for seventeen specific hands. For single and double deck games, you use the running count to vary the bet size and true count for the same seventeen playing situations.

2. To calculate the true count you must divide the running count by the number of unplayed decks of cards.

3. Estimate the number of unplayed decks of cards from the number of decks of cards in the discard tray. Therefore the number of unplayed decks of cards is simply the number of decks being used in the game minus the number of decks estimated in the discard tray.

4. Calculate the true count by dividing the running count by the number of unplayed decks of cards. In the case of single and double deck games, use the appropriate multiplier to make this conversion.

5. If your true count contains a fraction, round up for fractions greater than ½ and round down for fractions ½ or less.

6. In single deck games with no discard tray, use the correct multiplier based upon number of hands played.

Don't be alarmed by what first appears to be a complicated mathematical manipulation that needs to be done in your head while you play blackjack. Once you practice the conversion of running count to true count, it will become automatic. In reality, you'll have a number in your memory (the running count) which you'll quickly divide by another number to estimate the true count. The entire process, with a little practice, will take literally seconds. Remember we are not after scientific accuracy to two decimals. All we want to do is to make our best estimate as accurate as we can as to the composition of the remaining cards. With practice, you'll be able to make this conversion a lot easier than you think.

As mentioned earlier, we will use the technique of converting our running count to true count for sizing our bets in multiple (4, 6, 8) deck games and for deviating from basic strategy.

With single and double deck games, we'll use the running count to determine our bet size and the true count for strategy deviations.

Bet Sizing

You win money playing blackjack by betting more when you have the advantage and less when you don't. In general, your advantage increases by 0.5% for every one unit increase in the true count. Thus in multiple deck games where the casino typically has a 0.5% advantage over the player, you need a true count of +1 to be even and +2 to have a 0.5% advantage. The more positive the true count, the greater your advantage (likewise, the more negative the true count, the greater your disadvantage).

Whenever your count is negative, this indicates an unfavorable situation for the player and therefore warrants a small bet. When the count is positive, this is a player favorable situation and you will make a large bet. In essence you are using the count to make larger bets when you have the advantage and small (or no) bets when you don't.

There are several schools of thought regarding how to vary your bets based upon the count. At one extreme, you only bet when you have the advantage (positive count) and not bet at all in negative counts. This technique was made popular by Stanford Wong and is known as "Wonging." The other extreme is known as proportional betting. Here you size your bet in direct proportion to the true count. The greater the true count, the higher your advantage, and therefore the more you bet. The middle of the road technique for varying bets is to use qualitative bet sizing based upon the running count. Here, three levels of bets are made depending upon whether the running count is positive, negative or neutral.

I have found from my 25 years of playing blackjack that you will do just fine by using the running count for bet sizing in single and double deck games but with multiple deck games you'll need to learn proportional betting based upon the true count. The following recommended bet spread is based upon my experiences as to what the casinos will tolerate before they begin to scrutinize your play to determine if you are counting (I'll have more to say about this later).

Single Deck

I've used a 1 to 3 bet spread against the very favorable Las Vegas single deck games without problems for over 20 years. You vary your bets based upon the running count as follows:

Running Count	Bet Size
negative	1 unit
neutral (0)	2 units
positive	3 units

Betting in this manner means your first bet at the start of a new game is 2 units. After the first round is completed, you adjust your bet size either up, down or the same depending upon the count. Whenever the running count is negative, make your small bet (1 unit). Whenever the count is positive, bet more (3 units).

This is a simple and effective betting strategy for single deck games with good rules (Las Vegas). The bet spreads for various size minimum bets is summarized below:

Unit Bet	Bet Spread
$5	$5 to $15
$10	$10 to $30
$25	$25 to $75
$100	$100 to $300

I would also suggest that if the count gets very negative (-3 or worse) toward the end of the playing round, you sit out a few hands until the shuffle. You can usually get away with this without attracting too much attention from casino supervisors especially if you have been losing a few hands. If you happen to be winning consecutive hands and the count goes very negative, sitting out a few hands is an unnatural blackjack play (most gamblers sit out hands when they are losing to change their luck, not when winning). If you do it, do it only once during any one playing session.

If you use the above three level betting scheme, keep an accurate count and avoid betting in very negative counts, you'll have about a one and one half percent advantage over the casino.

In single deck games with less favorable rules (e.g. Reno rules), you need to use the two deck betting spread to get about the same advantage.

Double Deck Games

With double deck games, I recommend a 1 to 4 betting spread. The spread needs to be greater than single deck games to compensate for the added casino edge with two decks (vs. one). Vary your bets as follows:

Running Count	Bet Size
negative	1 unit
neutral (0)	2 units
positive	4 units

If the running count gets to -6 or worse, I'd again sit out a few hands and resume betting when the count gets better than -6. Be careful you don't use this technique of sitting out a few hands too often at the same playing session. This is another flag that casino executives look for in card counters. In this situation it's better to just leave the table if the count dips very negative and play elsewhere.

The above betting spread and avoiding making bets in very negative counts will give you about a one and one half percent advantage over the casino.

Multiple Deck Games

With 4, 6, or 8 deck games, you must convert the running count to true count for bet sizing. It is also very important to not make bets when the true count is -2 or worse.

Vary your bets as follows:

True Count	4 Decks	6 Decks	8 Decks
−1 to 0	1 unit	1 unit	1 unit
+1	2 units	2 units	3 units
+2	3 units	4 units	5 units
≥ +3	5 units	8 units	10 units

You need a larger betting spread the more decks the casino uses to compensate for their added advantage with multiple decks. If you want to maintain a one percent advantage, you must not continue to play and bet with large negative counts. This is extremely important especially in the 6 and 8 deck shoe games! In practical terms this means you should expect to do a lot of table hopping in multiple deck games.

Here are some additional pointers to keep in mind when varying your bets based upon the count.

1. It is to your advantage to play two hands rather than one when the true count becomes very positive and your bet size increases. Thus instead of playing one

hand of 8 units, it is better to play two hands with a 4 unit bet on each hand. Better yet, bet 3 units on one hand and 5 units on the other hand. This helps camouflage the fact that you've increased your bet from 4 to 8 units.

2. Casino supervisors understand that to win money at blackjack you must vary your bet size. Therefore, they become suspicious of players who make dramatic increases in the size of their bets, say $25 to $100, from one hand to the next. Therefore, be careful not to increase your bet size more than 2 to 3 units over your last bet unless you believe you can get away with it. The trick is to try to bet like a typical blackjack player. Most will parlay or double their bets after a win. If you've won a hand and the true count increased to indicate a larger bet, doubling the size of your bet is a natural play (for example from 5 to 10 units in an eight deck game). As long as you are winning hands, this technique of getting more money on the table will not attract attention. But what if you've lost a few bets and now the count jumps indicating a larger bet is in order? Most blackjack players don't increase their bets after a loss (except the most unskilled who double up trying to recoup losses as quickly as possible). Increasing your bet following a few losing hands is therefore not a natural blackjack play. But do as I do. I increase my bet but follow it with a few comments like, "I can't possibly lose another hand" or "I'm due to win this hand" or "There is no way you'll win another hand." Talk like this is typical of a blackjack player who is "steaming" his bets. Be careful not to do this play too often at one session. After the second time this happens, I usually will play a few more hands at the large bet (as long as the count remains positive) then leave the table.

3. What happens if you are winning your big bets and all of a sudden the count goes south indicating a small bet is in order. What I do in this situation is to drop immediately to my small bet but again follow it with a comment such as "It's time to lock up my winnings" or "I'd better lock up my profits before my luck turns." Remember, you want to give every indication that you are playing blackjack to have a good time not to win a lot of money.

4. A lot of card counters get caught with their pants down when they make a big bet and then the dealer unexpectedly reshuffles. Removing that big bet to place a small bet for the start of the next shoe (or deck) will definitely draw attention to your play. At least this is what my card counting friends tell me who get caught in this situation. I've never had this problem however, because I always pull back my winnings and original bet toward me and then after the round is over, make my next bet. It's a nice habit to develop.

5. Given the choice of playing alone (or head up) with the dealer vs. a table full of players, opt for the head up play. I never play single or double deck games with more than two other players. The reason is that I want to maximize the number of hands I get per hour (and mathematically, your win rate is slightly higher).

6. You really have two choices for bet size variation that will win you money. One is to vary your bet size in proportion to the advantage (or disadvantage) you have. The other is to simply never bet when you are at a disadvantage and just make big bets when you have the advantage. Stanford Wong, an expert player and one of the very best blackjack analysts and

writers, developed the technique of Wonging or back counting, which was published in his book, *Professional Blackjack*. I use back counting especially in the multiple deck games. To back count, you simply observe a game (after the shuffle) keeping the count (just stand behind a table and watch as an observer). When the count goes positive and you have the edge, jump in and start to play. When the count goes negative, leave the table and back count another table. This technique will give you the advantage with less of a betting spread than proportional betting. The bet size variation I recommend in this book uses a combination of bet variation on positive counts and no bet at all when the count gets real ugly (greater than true count of -1). I still back count prior to jumping in a game, and leave on negative counts. This style of play keeps me hopping from one table to another and sometimes from one casino to another. But I have learned over the years you are better off spending your time to find a game in which you have the advantage than biding your time making small bets in negative counts.

Back counting does draw attention from the pit especially if you do it often during a playing session. I'll have more to say about this in Chapter 8.

Deck Penetration

The casinos never deal all the cards at their blackjack tables. They generally will play with 50% to 80% of the cards. The amount of cards (or decks) that are put into play is known as the deck penetration.

As a general rule, the deeper the penetration (more decks put into play) the greater the advantage for the card counter. Playing at a blackjack table where the dealer cuts off 20% of the cards vs. 40% is a much better game. You want to seek games where the dealer places the cut card far back into the decks (or pack) of cards. This is good penetration and a better game.

Arnold Snyder has studied the effect of penetration in great detail. For example with a 1 to 4 betting spread in a typical 2 deck game with Las Vegas rules, the player's advantage (head up) varies with the penetration as follows:

50% penetration	+0.5% advantage
70% penetration	+1.0% advantage
90% penetration	+1.8% advantage

The bottom line here is to seek out games with good penetration (at least 75%) and definitely avoid games with lousy penetration. For example, when I played in the Atlantic City casinos after they first opened, deck penetration was very good (in fact, the Casino Control Commission regulated where the dealer could put the cut card). When rules changed in later years many casinos were using eight decks with a 50% penetration. This was an unbeatable game even for the card counter and for a long time I stopped playing blackjack until the penetration improved.

Bankroll Requirements

There are two terms you need to understand. The first is total bankroll which is a sum of money you will be using as capital to invest in playing blackjack. When you actually head off to the casinos, you'll take a portion of the total bankroll. This is known as your session stake.

One of the worst things that a blackjack card counter can do is to over bet in relation to his/her bankroll. Blackjack is a game of fluctuations which means even though you have the advantage and your bankroll will grow, it doesn't do so in a straight line. It's more of a roller coaster ride much like the stock market. Sometimes you'll win big, other times you'll lose big. If you can't stomach big losses than by God don't bet big.

To protect your bankroll against negative fluctuations (a series of losing sessions), you must have a proper ratio between your maximum bet and total bankroll. Mathematical equations can be used to calculate these ratios, but I'll get right down to the bottom line.

To ensure yourself a 95% chance of doubling your bankroll and less than 5% chance of losing it using the advanced card counting betting systems discussed in this chapter, you need to have 125 times your maximum bet as a total bankroll.

Size your session stake as follows. For short playing sessions (one or two days) bring 35 times your maximum bet. For long playing sessions, bring 50 times your maximum bet.

Let's put it all together in the form of a table to make it easy to understand this concept.

BANKROLL REQUIREMENTS

Betting Spread	Session Stake Short	Long	Total Bankroll
$2 to $8	$280	$400	$1,000
$5 to $20	$700	$1,000	$2,500
$10 to $50	$1,750	$2,500	$6,250
$25 to $100	$3,500	$5,000	$12,500
$100 to $400	$14,000	$20,000	$50,000

Betting more than the maximum bets listed above for the corresponding total bankroll will give you higher win rates but also a higher potential of losing it all. Do not make the fatal mistake of overbetting! Stay within the maximum bet to bankroll ratios listed above and you'll be avoiding the classic mistake of overbetting.

Remember that playing blackjack is risky even when you have the edge. I have personally experienced 10 consecutive losing sessions. By maintaining my cool and not overbetting, I never tapped out. Your bankroll will eventually grow especially when you learn to take the money (profits) and run, but always remember - it's a roller coaster ride to success.

For the serious reader who wants to learn more about the mathematics of risk/reward in relation to sizing a bankroll, I highly recommend Ken Uston's *Million Dollar Blackjack*, or Bryce Carlson's *Blackjack for Blood*.

Strategy Deviations

You can use the true count to not only vary your bets but also to alter your playing strategy. Blackjack computer software programs can be uscd to determine the value of the true count that a player should deviate from the basic playing strategy. These are known as strategy indices and charts containing these indices for the high low count can be found in blackjack books by Stanford Wong and Julian Braun. Dick Ramm and I have also independently calculated these strategy indices using a program developed by Dick.

When I first started playing serious blackjack I spent weeks memorizing tables of indices. I found I was making too many mistakes on the table trying to remember what to do when at what count. Then an article appeared in Arnold Snyder's *Blackjack Forum* newsletter, written by Donald Schlessinger.

Don calculated which strategy deviations give the player the most gain (about 90%) from varying from basic strategy. Surprisingly, it boiled down to just 18 strategy deviations. I threw away my table of indices and concentrated on learning just these deviations. Life at the blackjack tables has been much simpler for me ever since.

The most important strategy deviation is when to

take insurance. Do so when your true count is 1.5 or higher for single decks, 2.5 or higher for double decks, and 3 or more for multiple deck games.

When to Take Insurance

Game	True Count
Single Deck	1.5 or higher
Double Deck	2.5 or higher
4, 6, 8 Deck	3.0 or higher

When the dealer shows an ace upcard, you'll be asked whether or not you want to make the insurance bet. You must calculate the true count without any rounding to determine if insurance is a good bet. When your true count equals or exceeds the true count index listed above, take insurance. If it does not, than pass on the insurance bet.

The following table summarizes the indices for deviating from basic strategy for the plays listed. They were computed for multiple deck play but are close enough to use for single and double deck games.

You will follow one playing strategy when the true count exceeds the index number and an alternate strategy if it is equal to or less than the index number.

For example, if you are dealt a 16 and the dealer's upcard is a 10 you would stand if the true count equals +1 or exceeds +1 (the latter means +2, +3, +4, etc.). If the true count is less than +1 (0, −1, −2, etc.), follow the basic strategy and hit.

On negative indices, such as −1 when you hold 13 vs. dealer 2, you follow basic strategy and stand when true count is 0, +1, +2, +3, etc. You would deviate from basic strategy and hit if true count is −1, −2, −3, etc.

STRATEGY INDICES

Play	Index	Strategy
16 vs. 10	0	Stand at +1 and higher positive counts Hit at 0 and negative counts
15 vs. 10	+4	Stand at +5 and higher positive counts Hit at +4 and lower counts
10, 10 vs. 5	+5	Split at +6 and higher positive counts Stand at +5 and lower counts
10, 10 vs. 6	+4	Split at +5 and higher positive counts Stand at +4 and lower counts
10 vs. 10	+4	Double at +5 and higher positive counts Hit at +4 and lower counts
12 vs. 3	+2	Stand at +3 and higher positive counts Hit at +2 and lower counts
12 vs. 2	+3	Stand at +4 and higher positive counts Hit at +3 and lower counts
11 vs. Ace	+1	Double at +2 and higher positive counts Hit at +1 and lower counts
9 vs. 2	+1	Double at +2 and higher positive counts Hit at +1 and lower counts
10 vs. Ace	+4	Double at +5 and higher positive counts Hit at +4 and lower counts
9 vs. 7	+3	Double at +4 and higher positive counts Hit at +3 and lower counts
16 vs. 9	+5	Stand at +6 and higher positive counts Hit at +5 and lower counts
13 vs. 2	−1	Stand at 0 and positive counts Hit at −1 and more negative counts
12 vs. 4	0	Stand at +1 and higher positive counts Hit at 0 and more negative counts
12 vs. 6	−1	Stand at 0 and positive counts Hit at −1 and more negative counts

Notice that the range of indices listed in the table is +5 to −1. This is exactly the true count range that I play.

If you add up the above plays and throw in insurance, the total is 16. The two additional plays listed by Schlessinger that I've never used are 12 vs. 5 and 13 vs. 3 because the strategy index is −2 (I don't play when the true count is −2 so why learn this play).

By now you're probably asking yourself "how am I going to learn all this stuff." You have a lot more options than I did. The way I learned the above is to put the play on one side of an index card and the index number on the other side. Then I flipped through those index cards one at a time until I memorized the index number for the play. I would set aside those index cards that gave me trouble and concentrated on them. To this day, I still have these index cards and I still go through them before every casino trip.

If you own a personal computer, there is an easier way to learn and practice the above strategy deviations. I can recommend Stanford Wong's Blackjack Count Analyzer software program. With it you can learn how to count cards and practice the above strategy deviations in an efficient manner (for information on this program, see the Suggested Reading section at end of book).

Summary

To master the advanced level playing strategy presented in this chapter you must do the following:

1. Memorize the basic playing strategy.
2. Learn how to count the cards.
3. Use the running count to vary your bet size in single and double deck games.
4. Learn how to convert the running count to true count.
5. Use the true count for bet size variation in multiple deck games.
6. Also use the true count for varying your playing strategy and determining when to take insurance (for all games).

7. Avoid overbetting.
8. Avoid playing in negative counts.
9. Play like a loser; watch your jump in bet size; keep your playing sessions short.
10. Be happy and glad with small wins ("take the money and run").

In the next chapters we'll discuss three more important aspects of winning blackjack play, namely, the risks involved in playing blackjack, disguising your skills, and tips on how to force yourself to take your table profits (the money) and run!

7

Risks of Playing Blackjack

Even though you will have the edge over the casinos by card counting, this will not guarantee that you will win every time you play. In fact, fluctuations in your bankroll are quite normal and should be expected. It's important that you understand why this is so.

We can calculate how much we can expect to win playing blackjack by multiplying the number of hands dealt to us per hour times our mathematical advantage times our average bet times the length of play. For example if we average $10 per hand and play for 5 hours with a 1.5% advantage we should expect to win $60 (average 80 hands/hr).

$10 per hand x 80 hands/hr x 5 hrs x 1.5% = $60

However, even though we expect to win $60 after 5 hours of playing we rarely win exactly $60. In fact we usually win more than $60 or less than $60. This deviation from what was expected can be mathematically calculated.

It is known as the standard deviation.

The equation for the calculation of the standard deviation in blackjack is:

$$Standard\ Deviation = \frac{1.1}{\sqrt{N}}$$

N is the number of hands played. In our example we played 400 hands of blackjack (80 hands per hour times 5 hours). The standard deviation is simply the square root of 400 divided into 1.1.

$$Standard\ Deviation = \frac{1.1}{\sqrt{400}} = \frac{1.1}{20} = 0.055\ or\ 5.5\%$$

What this means is that the standard deviation for our 400 hands of blackjack is 5.5% or 22 units (5.5% of 400). If we bet $10 on each hand than one standard deviation is $220. To get the expected range add and subtract $220 from our expected win.

$$\$60 + \$220 = +\$280$$
$$\$60 - \$220 = -\$160$$

Being one standard deviation away from the expected value means that 68.3% of the time (or about two thirds) we will end up our 5 hour playing session in the range of +$280 to −$160. We expect to win $60 but shouldn't be surprised if we end up ahead up to $280 or behind up to $160.

Doubling the standard deviation will give us 95% confidence in predicting the range. If we do this our new range is

$$+\$500\ to\ -\$380$$

Note that we have just as much chance of winning

$500 as we do losing $380 after our 5 hour session. And 95% of the time we will end up within this range.

Let's take another look at the variations from expected win for a blackjack card counter who will play over a weekend with a betting range of $25 to $100 and with a 1.5% advantage. Let's assume he plays 1500 hands of blackjack over the weekend and his average bet is $50.

His total betting handle is 1500 x $50 = $75,000
His expected win is 1.5% x $75,000 − $1,125
The standard deviation for 1500 hands of blackjack is 42 units.

$$\frac{1.1}{\sqrt{1500}} = \frac{1.1}{38.7} = 0.028 \; or \; 2.8\% \; x \; 1500$$

The variance or range at two standard deviations is 5.6% x 1500 = 84 units x $50/unit = $4,200.

The amount our player could be ahead or behind is

$$\$1125 + \$4200 = +\$5325$$
$$\$1125 - \$4200 = -\$3075$$

The bottom line is that this player could be ahead up to $5,325 or behind up to $3,075. Losing $3,000 should not be unexpected! Likewise winning up to $5,000 is possible. The point is, 95% of the time that this player plays over a weekend (that's 19 out of 20 weekend trips) he/she will end up somewhere in the range of +$5,325 to −$3,075.

I hope you get the point of this exercise. Playing blackjack is risky because your bankroll will fluctuate. You could just as likely be ahead as you could be behind. This is why losing consecutive sessions can and most probably will happen.

Given these natural fluctuations which are part of the game of blackjack, how do we cope? First of all, we must have an adequate bankroll to see us through negative swings. This is the reason we size our bankroll based upon our maximum bet. Over betting is the cardinal sin for all blackjack players. Don't do it!! Secondly, you must be psychologically ready for these swings. It's tough losing several thousands of dollars over a month's play and most blackjack players can't handle these situations very well. Unfortunately, you need money to make money when you play blackjack and to win big you've got to expect to lose big. If losing large sums of money gives you the shakes, than don't bet large sums. Play for small stakes, much like I did when I started, until you can handle the emotional highs when losing. Also, by using the concepts of locking up your profits (taking the money and run) discussed in Chapter 9, you'll be playing a more conservative game, content to leave a session with your profits regardless of the count.

Playing blackjack is risky but if you play long enough with the strategies I covered in this book, the statistical advantage you have will assert itself and you will win more than you lose.

8

Disguising Your Skills

Casinos are in business to make money. They prefer to cater to players who know how to lose rather than to those that know how to win. They have, in fact, excluded or barred professional blackjack card counters because they see them as a threat to their bottom line.

Although a lot has been written on the subject of disguising your skills to prevent getting barred, I don't get too excited over it. I've been card counting and winning for over 25 years and have been asked only twice to stop playing and leave. Both of these incidents occurred in Atlantic City casinos (the old Brighton, now the Sands and Harrahs), but it was stupidity and greed on my part that caused the barring.

If you follow the guidelines I'm about to present, your chances of ever getting a lot of "heat from the pit" are very small.

1. Watch Your Betting Spread
   Casino managers know that the bigger the spread used by a card counter the greater will be his/her advantage.

They are quite sensitive to a blackjack player that jumps his/her bet from say $10 to $50 or more. They do, however, tolerate smaller bet spreads. Therefore, the simple rule here is to follow the advice I presented on bet size variation in this book and in general don't increase your bet by more than 2 or 3 units unless you are winning consecutive hands, the count is still positive, and you can disguise a big jump of say 5 units by "letting your winnings ride."

2. Play Like the Losers
    I never play for more than one hour at one table. Learn to play for short time periods and be happy with modest profits. Remember your goal at each session is to take the money and run!

3. Act Natural
    One of the reasons I was barred in Atlantic City was that I was concentrating so hard on watching the cards and keeping the count that I never said a word to anyone. Try to act natural and talk to the dealer and your fellow players from time to time. I usually make it a point to ask the dealer how lucky he/she's been when I arrive at the table. Or better yet I'll ask my fellow players. Also, after the shuffle and during the deal of the first round, I usually indulge in small talk (at this point, I haven't started to pick up my count).

Now what about that floor person or pit boss who saunters up to your table and either watches your play or strikes up a conversation. In my early days of playing blackjack, this used to scare the crap out of me. However, I've learned that there is nothing to fear as long as I watch my betting spread and respond to his/her small talk just like other players would do. If the conversation makes you lose the count, just flat bet your minimum bet until the next round.

Here are some additional actions that I have used from time to time to minimize any attention to my play:

- Act undecided on how to play a hand. Sometimes I'll ask for help from the dealer or fellow players. Appearing unsure of decisions will label you as a "dumb" player.
- Don't buy-in for large sums. Even at a $25 minimum table, my normal buy-in is $300-$400.
- When I'm winning big, I discretely place chips in my pocket.
- Instead of making one large bet on plus counts (e.g. $50), I generally make two uneven bets ($20 and $30) on two hands.
- Sometimes, but not often, when the count jumps very positive and I have a very strong feeling I'm being watched, I'll wait one more hand before increasing my bet and when I do, I place a pile of chips of different denominations as a bet (usually a green $25 chip on bottom, with a bunch of red $5 on top).
- When the count goes negative, I try to sit out a few hands and make the excuse "I want to change the luck of the table."

The bottom line is that you must play in a manner that does not draw attention to you. Act like the losers, dress like the losers, play smart, and above all, when you're ahead, learn to take the money and run!

9

Take the Money and Run

This is the most important chapter in this book. If you follow my advice you'll learn how to discipline yourself to take the profits you've earned through smart play and walk away a winner (i.e. take the money and run!).

I get sick every time I hear about someone being ahead a lot of money in the casinos and instead of pocketing at least some of the profits, continues to play and loses it all back. Think about how ridiculous this is. They come to win money and if they are skillful and lucky to get ahead, they keep playing and losing. It's crazy yet the casino managers depend upon this playing mentality to keep them in business. As one executive of a large casino once told me, "if every player would walk away when they get ahead, we'd be out of business."

So why do the vast majority of blackjack players do it? One reason is their objectives. They play blackjack "for the fun of it" and winning or losing is secondary. When these players get ahead, they wouldn't dream of quitting. They came for the action. And when they invariable lose it all back including their initial bankroll, they chalk up their losses to "bad luck." To make matters worse, they honestly believe that losing is the price you pay for an evening of fun and action. In fact, they enjoyed themselves so much, they'll come back and do it all over again, and again, and again.

If you ever expect to be a winning blackjack player, you must set a goal to never give back your hard earned profits to the casino. Always take the money and run!!

I have used and taught thousands of blackjack players the following techniques to help discipline themselves to walk away a winner. Sometimes this means stopping play after a relatively short time period. So be it. Winning a small profit is, you'll agree, better than no profit or a loss.

Your first objective when you buy-in at a blackjack table is to set a quitting milestone. If I buy in for 20 units, my first quitting milestone is 30 units. This simply means I am trying to "grow" my initial 20 unit bankroll to 30 units (i.e. 10 unit profit). If I'm successful, I then set a new quitting milestone of 40 units. As long as I keep winning and achieving a milestone, I keep increasing it by 10 units (i.e. 30, 40, 50, 60 etc. units). Now here is the key to walking away with profits. *If at any point during play my session bankroll drops below the last established quitting milestone, that's my cue to "take the money and run."*

Let's go over this concept with an example. Suppose you buy-in for $100 and set $150 as your first quitting milestone. As soon as you exceed $150, set your next quitting milestone at $200. As long as your bankroll exceeds $150, keep playing. If you exceed $200, then set a new quitting milestone at $250. Suppose your bankroll has grown to $230 and after losing a few hands, your bankroll drops below your last established quitting milestone of $200. Say after your last losing hand you have $185. This is the time to get up and leave. In fact, at any time your bankroll drops below your last established quitting milestone, this is your cue to take your money and run.

When you think about it, this concept puts no limit

on the amount that you can win per session. It also forces you to walk away with profits. It's the ideal concept to follow if you're serious about winning.

The difficulty in applying this concept will come when your count is positive, you lose a large bet, and even though the count is still positive your playing bankroll has dropped below the last quitting milestone. From a purely mathematical standpoint you still have the edge on the next hand and should bet. However, my goal is take the money and run. This superceeds everything else. I enjoy the drive home with money I won from the casinos. Even if the amount won is relatively small, psychologically I feel good and from my experience, these small profits add up over time. After all this was my objective when I sat down to play - to win money. And when I do, I run!

From a practical standpoint, I keep track of the status of my bankroll during play by stacking my chips into equal piles. For example, if I buy-in for $200 I stack my chips into four piles of $50. I set aside three piles and use one to bet with. When I'm winning, I keep stacking my winning chips into piles of $50. Every time I win $50 or more, I set aside that pile of chips next to the original three piles of $50 and play with the leftover chips. I always know the status of my bankroll by simply counting my piles of chips. Once I have achieved six piles of chips, I know I've reached my first quitting milestone of $300. If I continue to win, I keep stacking my chips into $50 piles. However, if I lose and drop below $300, I take the money and run.

By now you're probably asking, what happens when you sit down and rather than start winning, you start losing. Here again, I have a philosophy about being in a losing situation which I adhere to above all else. First, if I lose a maximum of 3 or 4 hands in a row, I'm gone from the table. I don't care if the count is plus one zillion. Three or four consecutive losing hands and I'm gone to find another table to play. Second, if I find myself gradually losing from the word go, I'll generally pick up and leave if I've lost 25% of my starting bankroll. In both of these situations, I take a walk around the casino blackjack tables looking for another opportunity to play my skills.

My criteria for table selection is quite simple. I want the least number of decks, good penetration, and a near empty table (maximum two other players). If I don't find such a game, I take a hike to the next casino. If I'm forced into playing a multiple deck shoe game because single or two decks are not offered, I always backcount and wait for a positive count before I "jump in" to a table in which it appears that the players are doing well. You can readily deduce this by glancing at the players' bankrolls and bet size. If the players are betting the minimum bet and don't have a lot of chips in front of them, what do you think is happening? Most likely, the dealer is beating the hell out of them. If I see this, I don't even bother to backcount that table. I look for tables in which players have a lot of chips in front of them and their bet size is greater than the table minimum. These are the tables I backcount in multiple deck games. When the count turns positive, I jump in and play. When it turns negative, especially in multiple deck games, I'm off to backcount another table.

Sometimes, no matter what you do, you lose hand after hand, table after table. Here's where the discipline really counts. In times like these I never ever lose more than my original starting bankroll without taking a break from the action. If I lose $200, I head for the pool, take a nap, see a show, have dinner, or whatever, but I don't keep playing. After my "break" I'll try again with another $200 playing bankroll.

When you play winning blackjack, it is also important that you don't let the casinos psych you into losing. From their perspective, they hate players who "take the money and run." When players get ahead, they want them to continue to play to get a shot at winning it back. You'll be supplied with "free" drinks, a comp for dinner or a show to take a break from the action (they expect you'll feel obligated to come back and play) and even a free room comp. With the latter the casino executives feel comfortable that you're still in "their place" and thus more likely to come down in the morning and play with those profits. Keep in mind that casino executives have the objective of separating you from your bankroll as quickly and painlessly as possible. They thrive on the turnover of players who know how to lose. And they go to great lengths to make players feel good about losing with their so-called comps. It always amazes me to see a blackjack player drop a couple of thousand dollars at the tables, and then given a free comp to the best restaurant in the house and a front row seat at the show. The chump wines and dines in the restaurant, goes to the show where invariably a lead off comedienne has him laughing and already forgetting about his thousand dollar losses, and finally entertained by a top named performer. What could be better than this, he thinks. This certainly is the good life. And within a couple of days, he's already making plans for his next foray into the casinos. A true loser and a player the casinos love and cater to.

Don't be like our chump. Play to win money and when you've got it, run!

10

Potpourri

This chapter contains some topics which every blackjack player should at least be aware of. The topics are not necessarily related so I'll cover each one separately.

Tipping the Dealer

Blackjack writers seem to get very emotional about this topic. Some, like Stanford Wong, rarely tip or toke dealers because "it is not cost effective." Others like Bryce Carlson and Donald Schlessinger do so because the dealers work hard, receive low pay, depend upon tips for their livelihood, and the majority of the time do indeed give good service.

I tend to agree with the latter. If a dealer is congenial and provides a relaxed, friendly playing atmosphere, I will make a tip bet on my hand especially if I'm winning. I normally convert a red five dollar chip into whites (one dollar) at the start of play. If I get good service from the dealer, I normally make a one or two dollar bet for them. If I win the hand, they'll win double the tip. If I lose, then the tip bet also loses, but the dealer usually is still apprecia-tive of my bet for them. I am cautious not to over tip and I certainly do not give the dealer my blackjack bonus payoff like a lot of players will do. I sometimes try to encourage dealers to give a good cut (deep penetration) by making a tip bet and saying something like "now that's a good cut." Sometimes this works (the dealer will continue to give a good cut knowing I'll bet for them), other times it doesn't. Certainly I don't tip dealers who seem to have gotten out of the wrong side of bed. I've had my fair share of them. But for the most part, dealers are friendly and deserve a tip for the service they provide. This is my opinion. You need to do what you believe is right for you.

Blackjack Teams

The late professional card counter, Ken Uston, used this technique to win hundreds of thousands of dollars from casino blackjack tables (see his book *Million Dollar Black-jack*). The concept involves a group of players combining individual bankrolls into one large bankroll (or bank). A group of players (usually 3 to 5) are taught the basic blackjack playing strategy and how to card count. Each member of the team is positioned at different blackjack tables. They make minimum bets and keep the count. Whenever the latter becomes favorable they use a hand signal to indicate this to a confederate (known as the big player). This player wanders around the casino waiting for the signal. He then approaches the table and immediately starts to make large bets (usually $100 and up) and contin-ues to do so until his partner indicates the count turned unfavorable (the playing partner does not increase his bet). The big player then leaves and waits for another signal from another confederate.

By playing in this manner, the big player never plays in negative counts and always makes large bets when he has the edge. The team also has a very large bet to bank ratio which is added protection against losing the bank. Also the average bet size is quite high which increases the expected hourly win rate. Overall, it's an ingenious technique to beat the casinos at blackjack.

I once was asked to participate on a blackjack team in Atlantic City. I went to a team meeting to get all the details. I didn't particularly feel comfortable about the other participants on the team so I didn't participate.

I like to be in control when I play blackjack. That's why I prefer to play alone. However, I have played on a "team" after my barring incident in Atlantic City. Here's how it worked. My wife sits at first base and plays perfect basic strategy. After a few minutes I come to the same table and generally sit away from her, never giving any indication we are married. I keep the count and always make a minimum bet. When the count is positive, I signalled her to go up in the bet size. She is talking, having a good time, and not watching the cards on the table like a counter does. Between the two of us, we are able to get very big bets out when we have the edge in a manner that draws no suspicion from the floor persons.

Casino Countermeasures

I've mentioned my barring incident. Usually this is the casino's last resort when they suspect a person is a card counter. More often then not, they usually will first do any of the following to suspected counters:

- shuffle up when the player makes a big bet
- move the cut card to the 50% level.

I've had both of these done to me on several occasions. No big deal. I just take a hike to another casino. (See Bill Zender's book, *Card Counting for the Casino Executive*, for an excellent discussion on this).

Other Playing Techniques

There have been other legal techniques developed to get the edge over the casino that do not involve card counting. Some of these techniques are controversial because they are difficult to analyze via computer studies. Other than Jerry Patterson's Target techniques (discussed below) I've never tried to learn these new techniques simply because I'm satisfied with my win performance with card counting.

- Observe the dealer's hole card. Sometimes dealers get sloppy and expose the value of their hole card when they peek. Players sitting at first base have the best shot at seeing the card (this is known as first basing). Sometimes the value of the down card can be seen by a player standing on the other side of the pit. This player then signals his confederate at the table (this is known as spooking). I find spooking a bit unethical yet I know there are players doing this all the time.

  Front Loading is a technique in which a player sitting in the middle of the table tries to catch the dealer's down card as the dealer delivers the card under his/her up card. This technique is only possible with sloppy dealers.

- Warps. Sometimes dealers will warp or bend the cards when they peek at their hole card. This can lead to tens and picture cards having a noticeable or readable warp that can be used by a player to his/her advantage.

- Tells. Sometimes dealers unconsciously give a signal or tell when they check their hole card. It could be a verbal tell (comments) or physical tell (body motion). If a player can read these dealer's tells it gives them the edge. The book, *Read the Dealer*, by Steve Forte describes this technique in great detail.

- <u>Shuffle Tracking</u>. This technique involves remembering the locations of slugs of tens and picture cards in the discard tray and then tracking these clumps or slugs through the shuffle. The player can then cut these cards into play. For details on this technique, see Jerry Patterson's book, *Blackjack. A Winners Handbook.*

- <u>Dealer/Player Biases</u>. Jerry Patterson and Eddie Olson developed a technique for selecting a player favorable blackjack table based upon 18 factors. These factors indicate whether the table is player biased or dealer biased caused by non random shuffling of the cards. They call this technique Target 21. For details, see Jerry's book listed above.

New Options

To increase player interest in blackjack, many casinos have recently started to offer new options and special payoffs. These are options and a casino may or may not offer them to the player.

Over-Under 13: This is a side bet that can be made by blackjack players in which they are betting that the total of their first two cards is either greater than or less than 13. For example, if you bet under 13 and your first two cards total 2 through 12, you win your bet (1 to 1 payoff). If your cards total 13 or higher, you lose the bet. Same rules for the over 13 bet except you are betting that the first two cards total over 13. Once the over/under bet is settled, the twenty one hand is played out.

Arnold Snyder has developed a specific card counting

system for the over/under bet. Please see the suggested readings for details on how to request information from Arnold.

Multiple Action Blackjack: This new blackjack game was created by the Four Queens Casino in downtown Las Vegas and is being licensed by them to other casinos. This game allows players to make three separate wagers on the same hand. After the dealer completes his hand for the first wager, the dealer keeps the upcard and completes a second hand against the players original hand. This is repeated a third time to determine the outcome of the third hand. Thus the player's hand is used for three games in which the dealer's upcard remains constant.

The casinos' hold on multiple action blackjack is slightly greater than regular blackjack because players tend to deviate from basic strategy to avoid losing three bets (if they bust for example). However, basic strategy should be strictly followed in this game. Since you are making two to three bets per hand, your risk is slightly greater than betting three simultaneous hands of blackjack.

Double Exposure Blackjack: This is another unique variation of blackjack in which both dealer cards are dealt face-up. However, because you can see both of the dealer's cards, the playing rules are modified. This includes paying black-jacks at 1 to 1 (except the A, J of diamonds is paid at 2 to 1), doubling down is only permitted on hands that total 9, 10, or 11 (doubling on soft hands is not permitted), surrender, insurance and resplits are not allowed and all tie hands result in a loss (except a player's blackjack beats a dealer's blackjack). Because of these rule changes, double exposure blackjack is not as favorable a game as the normal casino blackjack game.

If you want to play this game, you need to learn a modified basic strategy. Please consult Stanford Wong's book, *Basic Blackjack*, for details.

Five Card 21: Some casinos pay a bonus 2 to 1 payoff, if the player hand totals 21 in five cards.

Six Card Automatic Winner: If a player has six cards that total 21 or less, the hand is an automatic winner.

6,7,8: If a player gets a 21 with a 6,7,8 of the same suit, the player receives a 2 to 1 bonus payoff.

7,7,7: If a player gets a three card 7 hand (totaling 21), the player receives a 3 to 2 bonus payoff.

Red or Black: You wager on the color of the dealer's upcard. If you guess right you are paid even money. If the upcard is a deuce of the color you selected, this is a push or tie (you don't win or lose). This gives the casino a 3.8% advantage.

Royal Match: This is a side bet that players can make in which they are wagering that the initial two cards dealt to them will be the same suit. A bonus is paid for king and queen of the same suit (10 to 1 in a single deck game). The casino edge is about 4.0%.

　　　　Casinos continue to offer these side bets and special rules to encourage more players to their tables. Likewise, players will continue to develop new techniques to beat the game. To stay on top of this continuous change, you need to subscribe to a blackjack newsletter or gaming magazine. For details, see the Suggested Reading.

11

Summary

To become a winning blackjack player you need to do the following:

1. Learn the basic blackjack playing strategy.
2. Play only in games with favorable rules.
3. Learn to keep track of the cards.
4. Given a choice, play single or two deck games vs. multiple deck shoe games.
5. Increase your bet size when you have the edge.
6. Vary your playing strategy based upon the count.
7. Don't waste a lot of time playing in negative counts especially in multiple deck games.
8. Watch your betting spread.
9. Disguise your skills.

And finally, above all else, when the opportunity arises (and believe me it will) and you have piles of winning chips in front of you, *be smart*,

TAKE THE MONEY AND RUN!!

Suggested Reading

These are my favorite books. I can recommend them to anyone who wants to learn more about blackjack.

Fundamentals of Blackjack by Carlson Chambliss and Thomas Roginski. A concise yet very thorough survey of the entire field of blackjack.

Professional Blackjack by Stanford Wong. The bible for serious card counters.

Basic Blackjack by Stanford Wong. Contains an excellent explanation of basic strategy and the basic strategy for common and not so common rules.

Blackjack Secrets by Stanford Wong. Excellent tips on how to win without getting kicked out of the casino.

Card Counting for the Casino Executive by Bill Zender. Although written for casino executives, this book gives a good overview of what it takes to win at blackjack.

Read the Dealer by Steve Forte. The bible for recognizing dealer tells.

The Theory of Blackjack by Peter Griffin. Heavy in math but excellent study of the game of blackjack.

Blackjack. A Professional Manual by Michael Dalton. Excellent reference book on blackjack. Covers literally everything to do with the game.

Million Dollar Blackjack by Ken Uston. Contains excellent advice on card counting teams and Ken Uston's experience as a professional player.

Blackjack for Blood by Bryce Carlson. Another very good "bible" for serious blackjack players.

Blackjack. A Winners Handbook by Jerry Patterson. Presents new and often controversial techniques for winning at blackjack.

How To Play Winning Blackjack by Julian Braun. One of the best books to learn the basic playing strategy.

Playing Blackjack as a Business by Lawrence Revere. A classic book on blackjack although slightly outdated.

Beat the 1-Deck Game by Arnold Snyder. Gives good information on win rates for card counters. Similar information is contained in Arnold Snyder's other books: *Beat the 2-Deck Game, 4-Deck, 6-Deck, and 8-Deck Games.*

Beat the Dealer by Edward Thorp. Another classic and first book to present a card counting strategy to beat the casino game of blackjack.

Two other very useful books for casino players that I can recommend are:

Bargain City by Anthony Curtis. Excellent overview of how to get the best deals when visiting Las Vegas.

Casino/Resort Riverboat and Fun Book Guide by Steve Bourie. Handy guide with excellent overview of gaming in each state with names, addresses, telephone numbers of casinos, maps, description of each property and more.

These are my favorite newsletters on blackjack. Write for a sample copy and rates.

Blackjack Forum by Arnold Snyder. RGE Publishing, 414 Santa Clara Avenue, Oakland, CA 94610

Current Blackjack News by Stanford Wong. Pi Yee Press, 7910 Ivanhoe Avenue, La Jolla, CA 92037

Blackjack Review by Michael Dalton. Spur of the Moment Publishing, P.O. Box 541967, Merritt Island, FL 32954

Blackjack Monthly by Robert Gates. Richard Canfield Assoc., P.O. Box 2830, Escondido, CA 92025

The following magazines/newsletters regularly feature articles on blackjack:

Casino Player, 2524 Arctic Avenue, Atlantic City, NJ 08401

Casino Magazine, 115 South State Street, Waseca, MN 56093

Las Vegas Advisor, P.O. Box 28041, Las Vegas, NV 89126

The Card Player, 1455 E. Tropicana Ave #450, Las Vegas, NV 89119

Blackjack Computer Software
I can highly recommend Blackjack Count Analyzer by Stanford Wong (to learn card counting) and Dr. Thorp's Mini Blackjack for learning just basic strategy. There are other blackjack software programs available. If you'd like to learn more about these programs, I suggest you purchase the December 1993 issue of Arnold Snyder's *Blackjack Forum*. Arnold reviews several different types of blackjack software programs in the issue.

A complete catalog containing the above products plus hundreds of other books on gambling can be obtained from these sources:

Gamblers Book Club, Las Vegas 1-800-634-6243
Gamblers General Store, Las Vegas 1-800-332-2447

APPENDIX I

BASIC

STRATEGY CHARTS

Chart 1

Multiple Deck Basic Strategy
Dealer stands on soft 17
Doubling on any two cards
Doubling after pair splitting permitted

Dealer's Upcard

Your Hand	2	3	4	5	6	7	8	9	10	A
17	S	S	S	S	S	S	S	S	S	S
16	S	S	S	S	S	H	H	H*	H*	H*
15	S	S	S	S	S	H	H	H	H*	H
14	S	S	S	S	S	H	H	H	H	H
13	S	S	S	S	S	H	H	H	H	H
12	H	H	S	S	S	H	H	H	H	H
11	D	D	D	D	D	D	D	D	D	H
10	D	D	D	D	D	D	D	D	H	H
9	H	D	D	D	D	H	H	H	H	H
8	H	H	H	H	H	H	H	H	H	H
A,8	S	S	S	S	S	S	S	S	S	S
A,7	S	D	D	D	D	S	S	H	H	H
A,6	H	D	D	D	D	H	H	H	H	H
A,5	H	H	D	D	D	H	H	H	H	H
A,4	H	H	D	D	D	H	H	H	H	H
A,3	H	H	H	D	D	H	H	H	H	H
A,2	H	H	H	D	D	H	H	H	H	H
A,A	P	P	P	P	P	P	P	P	P	P
10,10	S	S	S	S	S	S	S	S	S	S
9,9	P	P	P	P	P	S	P	P	S	S
8,8	P	P	P	P	P	P	P	P	P	P
7,7	P	P	P	P	P	P	H	H	H	H
6,6	P	P	P	P	P	H	H	H	H	H
5,5	Always Treat as 10, never Split									
4,4	H	H	H	P	P	H	H	H	H	H
3,3	P	P	P	P	P	P	H	H	H	H
2,2	P	P	P	P	P	P	H	H	H	H

*Surrender if offered

S= STAND   H= HIT   D= DOUBLE   P= SPLIT

Chart 2   **133**

Multiple Deck Basic Strategy
Dealer stands on soft 17
Doubling on any two cards
Doubling after pair splitting *not* permitted

Dealer's Upcard

Your Hand	2	3	4	5	6	7	8	9	10	A
17	S	S	S	S	S	S	S	S	S	S
16	S	S	S	S	S	H	H	H*	H*	H*
15	S	S	S	S	S	H	H	H	H*	H
14	S	S	S	S	S	H	H	H	H	H
13	S	S	S	S	S	H	H	H	H	H
12	H	H	S	S	S	H	H	H	H	H
11	D	D	D	D	D	D	D	D	D	H
10	D	D	D	D	D	D	D	D	H	H
9	H	D	D	D	D	H	H	H	H	H
8	H	H	H	H	H	H	H	H	H	H
A,8	S	S	S	S	S	S	S	S	S	S
A,7	S	D	D	D	D	S	S	H	H	H
A,6	H	D	D	D	D	H	H	H	H	H
A,5	H	H	D	D	D	H	H	H	H	H
A,4	H	H	D	D	D	H	H	H	H	H
A,3	H	H	H	D	D	H	H	H	H	H
A,2	H	H	H	D	D	H	H	H	H	H
A,A	P	P	P	P	P	P	P	P	P	P
10,10	S	S	S	S	S	S	S	S	S	S
9,9	P	P	P	P	P	S	P	P	S	S
8,8	P	P	P	P	P	P	P	P	P	P
7,7	P	P	P	P	P	P	H	H	H	H
6,6	H	P	P	P	P	H	H	H	H	H
5,5	Always Treat as 10, never Split									
4,4	H	H	H	H	H	H	H	H	H	H
3,3	H	H	P	P	P	P	H	H	H	H
2,2	H	H	P	P	P	P	H	H	H	H

*Surrender if offered

S= STAND   H= HIT   D= DOUBLE   P=SPLIT

Chart 3
Multiple Deck Basic Strategy
Dealer stands on soft 17
Doubling only on 10 and 11
Doubling after pair splitting *not* permitted

Your Hand	Dealer's Upcard									
	2	3	4	5	6	7	8	9	10	A
17	S	S	S	S	S	S	S	S	S	S
16	S	S	S	S	S	H	H	H*	H*	H*
15	S	S	S	S	S	H	H	H	H*	H
14	S	S	S	S	S	H	H	H	H	H
13	S	S	S	S	S	H	H	H	H	H
12	H	H	S	S	S	H	H	H	H	H
11	D	D	D	D	D	D	D	D	D	H
10	D	D	D	D	D	D	D	D	H	H
A,A	P	P	P	P	P	P	P	P	P	P
10,10	S	S	S	S	S	S	S	S	S	S
9,9	P	P	P	P	P	S	P	P	S	S
8,8	P	P	P	P	P	P	P	P	P	P
7,7	P	P	P	P	P	P	H	H	H	H
6,6	H	P	P	P	P	H	H	H	H	H
5,5	Always Treat as 10, never Split									
4,4	H	H	H	H	H	H	H	H	H	H
3,3	H	H	P	P	P	P	H	H	H	H
2,2	H	H	P	P	P	P	H	H	H	H

*Surrender if offered
S= STAND   H= HIT   D= DOUBLE   P=SPLIT

A,2 through A,6 always *hit.*
A,8 through A,10 always *stand.*
A,7 *hit* on dealer's 9, 10, A and *stand* on 2 through 8.

Chart 4 135

Single Deck Basic Strategy
Dealer stands on soft 17
Doubling on any two cards
Doubling after pair splitting *not* permitted

Dealer's Upcard

Your Hand	2	3	4	5	6	7	8	9	10	A
17	S	S	S	S	S	S	S	S	S	S
16	S	S	S	S	S	H	H	H	H*	H
15	S	S	S	S	S	H	H	H	H*	H
14	S	S	S	S	S	H	H	H	H	H
13	3	3	3	3	3	H	H	H	H	H
12	H	H	S	S	S	H	H	H	H	H
11	D	D	D	D	D	D	D	D	D	D
10	D	D	D	D	D	D	D	D	H	H
9	D	D	D	D	D	H	H	H	H	H
5,3	H	H	H	D	D	H	H	H	H	H
A,8	S	S	S	S	D	S	S	S	S	S
A,7	S	D	D	D	D	S	S	H	H	H
A,6	D	D	D	D	D	H	H	H	H	H
A,5	H	H	D	D	D	H	H	H	H	H
A,4	H	H	D	D	D	H	H	H	H	H
A,3	H	H	D	D	D	H	H	H	H	H
A,2	H	H	D	D	D	H	H	H	H	H
A,A	P	P	P	P	P	P	P	P	P	P
10,10	S	S	S	S	S	S	S	S	S	S
9,9	P	P	P	P	P	S	P	P	S	S
8,8	P	P	P	P	P	P	P	P	P	P
7,7	P	P	P	P	P	P	H	H	S*	H
6,6	P	P	P	P	P	H	H	H	H	H
5,5	Always Treat as 10, never Split									
4,4	H	H	H	D	D	H	H	H	H	H
3,3	H	H	P	P	P	P	H	H	H	H
2,2	H	P	P	P	P	P	H	H	H	H

*Surrender if offered
S= STAND   H= HIT   D= DOUBLE   P=SPLIT

Chart 5

<u>Single Deck Basic Strategy</u>
Dealer stands on soft 17
Doubling on any two cards
Doubling after pair splitting permitted

Dealer's Upcard

Your Hand	2	3	4	5	6	7	8	9	10	A
17	S	S	S	S	S	S	S	S	S	S
16	S	S	S	S	S	H	H	H	H*	H
15	S	S	S	S	S	H	H	H	H*	H
14	S	S	S	S	S	H	H	H	H	H
13	S	S	S	S	S	H	H	H	H	H
12	H	H	S	S	S	H	H	H	H	H
11	D	D	D	D	D	D	D	D	D	D
10	D	D	D	D	D	D	D	D	H	H
9	D	D	D	D	D	H	H	H	H	H
5,3	H	H	H	D	D	H	H	H	H	H
A,8	S	S	S	S	D	S	S	S	S	S
A,7	S	D	D	D	D	S	S	H	H	H
A,6	D	D	D	D	D	H	H	H	H	H
A,5	H	H	D	D	D	H	H	H	H	H
A,4	H	H	D	D	D	H	H	H	H	H
A,3	H	H	D	D	D	H	H	H	H	H
A,2	H	H	D	D	D	H	H	H	H	H
A,A	P	P	P	P	P	P	P	P	P	P
10,10	S	S	S	S	S	S	S	S	S	S
9,9	P	P	P	P	P	S	P	P	S	S
8,8	P	P	P	P	P	P	P	P	P	P
7,7	P	P	P	P	P	P	P	H	S*	H
6,6	P	P	P	P	P	P	H	H	H	H
5,5	Always Treat as 10, never Split									
4,4	H	H	P	P	P	H	H	H	H	H
3,3	P	P	P	P	P	P	H	H	H	H
2,2	P	P	P	P	P	P	H	H	H	H

*Surrender if offered

S= STAND   H= HIT   D= DOUBLE   P= SPLIT

Chart 6   **137**

Single Deck Basic Strategy
Dealer stands on soft 17
Doubling only on 10 and 11
Doubling after pair splitting *not* permitted

Dealer's Upcard

Your Hand	2	3	4	5	6	7	8	9	10	A
17	S	S	S	S	S	S	S	S	S	S
16	S	S	S	S	S	H	H	H	H*	H
15	S	S	S	S	S	H	H	H	H*	H
14	S	S	S	S	S	H	H	H	H	H
13	S	S	S	S	S	H	H	H	H	H
12	H	H	S	S	S	H	H	H	H	H
11	D	D	D	D	D	D	D	D	D	D
10	D	D	D	D	D	D	D	D	H	H
A,A	P	P	P	P	P	P	P	P	P	P
10,10	S	S	S	S	S	S	S	S	S	S
9,9	P	P	P	P	P	S	P	P	S	S
8,8	P	P	P	P	P	P	P	P	P	P
7,7	P	P	P	P	P	P	H	H	S*	H
6,6	P	P	P	P	P	H	H	H	H	H
5,5			Always Treat as 10, never split							
4,4	H	H	H	H	H	H	H	H	H	H
3,3	H	H	P	P	P	P	H	H	H	H
2,2	H	P	P	P	P	P	H	H	H	H

*Surrender if offered

S= STAND   H= HIT   D= DOUBLE   P=SPLIT

A,2 through A,6 always *hit.*

A,8 through A,10 always *stand.*

A,7 *hit* on dealer's 9, 10, A and *stand* on 2 through 8.

Chart 7

Single Deck Basic Strategy
Dealer hits soft 17
Doubling only on 10 and 11
Doubling after pair splitting *not* permitted

Dealer's Upcard

Your Hand	2	3	4	5	6	7	8	9	10	A
17	S	S	S	S	S	S	S	S	S	S
16	S	S	S	S	S	H	H	H	H	H
15	S	S	S	S	S	H	H	H	H	H
14	S	S	S	S	S	H	H	H	H	H
13	S	S	S	S	S	H	H	H	H	H
12	H	H	S	S	S	H	H	H	H	H
11	D	D	D	D	D	D	D	D	D	D
10	D	D	D	D	D	D	D	D	H	H
A,A	P	P	P	P	P	P	P	P	P	P
10,10	S	S	S	S	S	S	S	S	S	S
9,9	P	P	P	P	P	S	P	P	S	P
8,8	P	P	P	P	P	P	P	P	P	P
7,7	P	P	P	P	P	P	H	H	S	H
6,6	P	P	P	P	P	H	H	H	H	H
5,5	Always Treat as 10, never Split									
4,4	H	H	H	H	H	H	H	H	H	H
3,3	H	H	P	P	P	P	H	H	H	H
2,2	H	H	P	P	P	P	H	H	H	H

S= STAND   H= HIT   D= DOUBLE   P= SPLIT

A,2 through A,6 always *hit.*
A,8 through A,10 always *stand.*
A,7 *hit* on dealer's 9, 10, A and *stand* on 2 through 8.

Chart 8   139

Double Deck Basic Strategy
Dealer stands on soft 17
Doubling on any two cards
Doubling after pair splitting *not* permitted

Your Hand — Dealer's Upcard

Your Hand	2	3	4	5	6	7	8	9	10	A
17	S	S	S	S	S	S	S	S	S	S
16	S	S	S	S	S	H	H	H	H*	H*
15	S	S	S	S	S	H	H	H	H*	H
14	S	S	S	S	S	H	H	H	H	H
13	S	S	S	S	S	H	H	H	H	H
12	H	H	S	S	S	H	H	H	H	H
11	D	D	D	D	D	D	D	D	D	H
10	D	D	D	D	D	D	D	D	H	H
9	D	D	D	D	D	H	H	H	H	H
5,3	H	H	H	H	H	H	H	H	H	H
A,8	S	S	S	S	S	S	S	S	S	S
A,7	S	D	D	D	D	S	S	H	H	H
A,6	H	D	D	D	D	H	H	H	H	H
A,5	H	H	D	D	D	H	H	H	H	H
A,4	H	H	D	D	D	H	H	H	H	H
A,3	H	H	H	D	D	H	H	H	H	H
A,2	H	H	H	D	D	H	H	H	H	H
A,A	P	P	P	P	P	P	P	P	P	P
10,10	S	S	S	S	S	S	S	S	S	S
9,9	P	P	P	P	P	S	P	P	S	S
8,8	P	P	P	P	P	P	P	P	P	P
7,7	P	P	P	P	P	P	H	H	H	H
6,6	P	P	P	P	P	H	H	H	H	H
5,5	Always Treat as 10, never Split									
4,4	H	H	H	H	H	H	H	H	H	H
3,3	H	H	P	P	P	P	H	H	H	H
2,2	H	H	P	P	P	P	H	H	H	H

*Surrender if offered
S= STAND   H= HIT   D= DOUBLE   P=SPLIT

Chart 9

Double Deck Basic Strategy
Dealer stands on soft 17
Doubling on any two cards
Doubling after pair splitting permitted

Your Hand / Dealer's Upcard

Your Hand	2	3	4	5	6	7	8	9	10	A
17	S	S	S	S	S	S	S	S	S	S
16	S	S	S	S	S	H	H	H	H*	H*
15	S	S	S	S	S	H	H	H	H*	H
14	S	S	S	S	S	H	H	H	H	H
13	S	S	S	S	S	H	H	H	H	H
12	H	H	S	S	S	H	H	H	H	H
11	D	D	D	D	D	D	D	D	D	H
10	D	D	D	D	D	D	D	D	H	H
9	D	D	D	D	D	H	H	H	H	H
5,3	H	H	H	H	H	H	H	H	H	H
A,8	S	S	S	S	S	S	S	S	S	S
A,7	S	D	D	D	D	S	S	H	H	H
A,6	H	D	D	D	D	H	H	H	H	H
A,5	H	H	D	D	D	H	H	H	H	H
A,4	H	H	D	D	D	H	H	H	H	H
A,3	H	H	H	D	D	H	H	H	H	H
A,2	H	H	H	D	D	H	H	H	H	H
A,A	P	P	P	P	P	P	P	P	P	P
10,10	S	S	S	S	S	S	S	S	S	S
9,9	P	P	P	P	P	S	P	P	S	S
8,8	P	P	P	P	P	P	P	P	P	P
7,7	P	P	P	P	P	P	H	H	H	H
6,6	P	P	P	P	P	H	H	H	H	H
5,5	Always Treat as 10, never Split									
4,4	H	H	H	P	P	H	H	H	H	H
3,3	P	P	P	P	P	P	H	H	H	H
2,2	P	P	P	P	P	P	H	H	H	H

*Surrender if offered

S= STAND   H= HIT   D= DOUBLE   P=SPLIT

APPENDIX II

BLANK BASIC STRATEGY CHART

Dealer's Upcard

Your Hand	2	3	4	5	6	7	8	9	10	A
17										
16										
15										
14										
13										
12										
11										
10										
9										
5,3										
A,8										
A,7										
A,6										
A,5										
A,4										
A,3										
A,2										
A,A										
10,10										
9,9										
8,8										
7,7										
6,6										
5,5										
4,4										
3,3										
2,2										

*Surrender if offered

S= STAND   H= HIT   D= DOUBLE   P=SPLIT

141

INDEX

About the Author

Henry Tamburin has been actively involved in casino gambling for the past 27 years as a player, author, instructor, and columnist. He has operated a casino gambling school to teach winning techniques to the public, written and published a newsletter on Atlantic City casino gambling and operated a club for casino players. He has written over 500 articles on casino gambling that have appeared in every major gaming magazine. His "how to win" seminars are well received by clubs/organizations. Henry has appeared on TV and radio and his exploits as a winning casino player and public educator have been featured in several newspaper stories. Most recently he is featured in the new instructional videos *Blackjack - Deal Me In* and *Craps - Rolling To Win*.

His books include: *Blackjack: Take the Money and Run, Craps: Take the Money and Run, Reference Guide to Casino Gambling Second Edition, The Ten Best Casino Bets Second Edition, Winning Baccarat Strategies, WBS Chart Book, Henry Tamburin on Casino Gambling, Casino Gambler's Survival Book, Casino Gambler's Quiz Book,* and *Pocket Guide to Casino Gambling*.

Henry Tamburin is a graduate of Seton Hall University with a Bachelor of Science degree in Chemistry, and the University of Maryland with a Doctor of Philosophy degree in Organic Chemistry. He works for a large international chemical company. He and his wife Linda have two grown sons.

Get 24 years of blackjack experience in just 90 minutes!

If you like Henry Tamburin's books on gambling, wait until you get your copy of his video! That's right, now you can watch Tamburin in action on video tape. In his video, "**Blackjack - Deal Me In**", he'll show you everything you need to know about blackjack. In this information packed tape, you'll learn:

• How to communicate with the casino like a pro.
• Where your best bets are
• How to manage your playing bankrolls,
• and what pitfalls to avoid.

You'll want to watch this information packed video tape again and again. There is simply too much to learn in one viewing.

So arm yourself with the knowledge you need to walk away from the casino a winner. Order your tapes today! And when you order your videos be sure to include the coupon below and your original sales receipt for any of Henry Tamburin's books. With your tapes, we'll send you the Blackjack Basic Strategy Card, a $3 value, free of charge!